Balance

dream,

   Know that your influence (I knew of you before I knew you) helped in this effort. I appreciate your example, love your mind and am always looking forward to your writing.

   Peace to You,

ADDITIONAL PRAISE FOR *BALANCE*

"In this engaging and overdue work, David Wall Rice develops a theoretical strategy for achieving more respectful and insightful understandings of the situated dynamics and agendas of identity-constitution and identity-maintenance—identity stasis—of African American male adolescents. With such understandings should come recognition and appreciation of the positive accomplishments and tremendous potential of this much maligned, often troubled, too frequently at-risk segment of the U.S. American population."

—**Lucius Turner Outlaw Jr.**, associate provost for undergraduate education and professor of philosophy, Vanderbilt University, and author of *Critical Social Theory in the Interests of Black Folks*

"This book presents a masterful discussion of the cultural and racial identity of young African American males. Rice uses a strengths-based approach to explore the concept of human identity through group sessions with six African American male teenagers. The author listens carefully to the voices of these young men as they struggle for authenticity and balance in their lives as they are consistently confronted by negative stereotypes of themselves. Rice provides a valuable analysis of a group rarely understood by most Americans."

—**Freeman A. Hrabowski III**, president, University of Maryland Baltimore County

Balance

Advancing Identity Theory by Engaging the Black Male Adolescent

DAVID WALL RICE

LEXINGTON BOOKS

A division of
ROWMAN & LITTLEFIELD PUBLISHERS, INC.
Lanham • Boulder • New York • Toronto • Plymouth, UK

LEXINGTON BOOKS

A division of Rowman & Littlefield Publishers, Inc.
A wholly owned subsidiary of The Rowman & Littlefield Publishing Group, Inc.
4501 Forbes Boulevard, Suite 200
Lanham, MD 20706

Estover Road
Plymouth PL6 7PY
United Kingdom

Copyright © 2008 by Lexington Books

All rights reserved. No part of this publication may be reproduced, stored in a retrieval system, or transmitted in any form or by any means, electronic, mechanical, photocopying, recording, or otherwise, without the prior permission of the publisher.

British Library Cataloguing in Publication Information Available

Library of Congress Cataloging-in-Publication Data

Rice, David Wall.
 Balance : advancing identity theory by engaging the black male adolescent / David Wall Rice.
     p. cm.
  Includes bibliographical references and index.
  ISBN-13: 978-0-7391-1888-7 (cloth : alk. paper)
  ISBN-10: 0-7391-1888-9 (cloth : alk. paper)
  1. African American teenage boys. 2. Teenage boys—Social conditions. 3. Minority teenagers—Social conditions. 4. African Americans—Race identity. 5. Adolescent psychology. I. Title.
   E185.86.R49 2008
   155.5'3208997—dc22   2007041344

Printed in the United States of America

™ The paper used in this publication meets the minimum requirements of American National Standard for Information Sciences—Permanence of Paper for Printed Library Materials, ANSI/NISO Z39.48–1992.

For Biko

Contents

Foreword Edmund W. Gordon, Ed.D.	xi
Preface	xv
Acknowledgments	xvii
Introduction: Contributions of Identity Stasis to Personality Psychology Cynthia E. Winston, Ph.D.	1
1 Thinking toward Theory	7
2 Underpinnings	19
3 Model Development: Placing Constructs	39
4 Orchestration	55
5 Beginning	67
Epilogue	77
Appendix 1	79
Appendix 2	89
Appendix 3	91
Appendix 4	95
Selected Bibliography	97
Index	115
About the Author	117

Then the wisest among them will say: What we have sought we have found, our own sense of identity. We have an established center out of which at last we can function and relate to other men. We have committed to heart and to nervous system a feeling of belonging and our spirits are no longer isolated and afraid. We have lost our fear of our brothers and are no longer ashamed of ourselves, of who and what we are—Let us now go forth to save the land of our birth from the plague that first drove us into the "will to quarantine" and to separate ourselves behind self-imposed walls. For this is why we were born: Men, all men belong to each other, and he who shuts himself away diminishes himself, and he who shuts another away from him destroys himself. And all the people said Amen.

Howard Thurman (1971)

FOREWORD

It was at the beginning of the twentieth century that W. E. B. Du Bois introduced into the lexicon of the social sciences concern for the possibility of a conflict in the sense of personal identity in persons who had been freed from centuries of enslavement, less than twenty-five years before. The sense of conflict or discord was between identity as a human being of African descent whose identity had been so dehumanized and denied by the enslavement and identity as a an American, membership in a group that had been and continued to be the instrument of this dehumanization.

> It is a peculiar sensation this double-consciousness, this sense of always looking at oneself through the eyes of others, of measuring one's soul by the tape of a world that looks on with amused contempt and pity. One ever feels his twoness, —an American, a Negro; two souls, two thoughts, two unreconciled strivings; two warring ideals in one dark body, whose dogged strength alone keeps it from being torn asunder, *Souls of Black Folks*, W. E. B. Du Bois 1903 p. 9.

In more recent years, the behavioral sciences have come to recognize and appreciate important differences in the functions of social identification and personal identity—identity as assigned by others and identity as self attribution—my personal belief concerning who I am and how I identify myself. As with the construction "Culture," we have also come to realize that the characteristics by which both culture and identity are associated are dynamic, fluid and unstable, despite their constancy. Thus it is that the components of each and their orchestrations change with time and situation, despite the colloquial notion that people can be described as being typical of a cultural group or as having the identity of a specific group. The implication of this misconceived notion is that cultures and identities are more or less fixed and stable phenomena.

As greater attention has come to be given to the co-existence of diverse groups of persons in the same geographic area, the Du Bosian notion of dual consciousness has gained in popularity. People are woman and American, of European descent and American, immigrants and American, ex-enslaved persons and American. Persons with such multiple identities are all around us. For some purposes we identify them as Americans. For other purposes we identify them by their more unique characteristics or histories. The same tends to be true of self identity except that there does appear to be a high degree of consistency in the core identity of self. Problems arise when the process of identification focuses exclusively on narrowly unique and often negative characteristics and function as stereotypes. The fact that African American males have been so stereotyped is one of the problems addressed in this book on "identity stasis."

Rice sees the stability of the core identity as a positive factor in the development of African American males and as an antidote to the ubiquitous negative stereotypes concerning this population.

In Identity Stasis Rice is not alone concerned with the distortions reflected in such stereotypes and their reduced capacity to inform our understanding of African American males. He is critical of this distorted identification by others and casts his work in the context of the personality psychology of identity formation and the dynamics of self identity. From this perspective, he rejects the pathology of stereotypical black experience to examine a wide range of behavioral adaptation in the service of the determination and exercise of one's identity utilizing personal narratives and discourse analysis as his investigative tools. Rice postulates that the "constellation of self-systems provides a tapestry by which identity theorists illustrate subjects' active striving for psychological balance." Identity is offered as one of the instruments by which the person is able to coordinate behavior that is adaptive to internal and external stimuli in effort directed at the establishment and maintenance of equilibrium. When Rice applies this conception to racial identity he considers the phenomenon a specialized, racialized form of identity stasis.

In their book *Goodness of Fit*, Stella Chess and Alexander Thomas; Brunner and Mazel 1999, introduce the physiological notion of homeostasis as a psychiatric term borrowed from the biological construct homeostasis. In both biology and psychology scientists are referencing the critical importance to life of the achievement and maintenance of stable balance in function as the optimal condition in living organisms. In Chess and Thomas's lexicon, the goal is to establish balance between the characteristics of the person and the characteristics of the effective environment—aspects of the environment that have relevance for the operative or targeted characteristics of the person. In biology homeostasis usually refers to balance within the organism, that is, balance between the several factors that constitute the living system. In living things, the loss of homeostasis is inconsistent with health and can lead to death. In psychiatry, the loss of homeostasis results in psychological malfunction and at worst mental illness.

In this book, Rice is concerned with issues having to do with cultural/racial identity as a phenomenon in the development of African American males. Although he has taken his focus on a population that too often is defined by its deficits, Rice has set his sights on advancing our understanding of universal issues concerning the development and function of identity in human subjects. At the core of Rice's concerns are three dynamic expressions of identity stasis:

1. identity dilemma articulation;
2. unadulterated presentation of self; and
3. burden of proof assumption.

In the *articulation mechanism*, Rice sees in his subjects the struggle with the paradox of incongruous striving to represent oneself as the same person but from dual and often competing models. Through the *unadulterated mechanism* the task is to represent oneself as one truly is—as though identity were veridical, that is, one or the other. In the mechanism represented by *burden of proof* the task is to represent oneself as the confirmation or disconfirmation of a socially constructed notion of the self as defined by others. Identity stasis appears to be the product of the individual's efforts at the orchestration of these three mechanisms. This appears to be a complementary construction of the mechanism identified by Chess and Thomas as "goodness of fit" in which the challenge to behavioral integration, maturity and health is the achievement and maintenance of homeostasis. Whether we are speaking of cultural identity, mental health, physical well being or racial identity the capacity to orchestrate different and often competing manifestations of dynamic life phenomena is an essential feature of human agency. Some of us argue that the behavior of African American males, like that of all living things, is a reflection of that struggle, some times made more difficult by hostile environments. Rice makes the case for these assertions beautifully in this book.

Edmund W. Gordon, Ed.D.
John M. Musser Professor of Psychology, Emeritus,
Yale University, and Richard March Hoe Professor of
Psychology and Education, Emeritus, Teachers College,
Columbia University

PREFACE

> Sources of theory range from intellectual to empirical to personal to group to worldview and, traditionally, the field has valued them in that sequence. Arguably, however, the less formal origins lead to at least equally impactful theory because they are more provocative and heuristic.
>
> Fiske, 2004

For many Black males there is not a question of success, rather a question of the type of success that they will occupy. My mother and father set as cornerstone of my development that I was special and that there were imperatives to being special; namely practiced faith, work, sacrifice and commitment to community. These fundamentals informed the context of my development and are in the main of how our society appreciates successful people.

I start with my life as example because it is normal. The precedent that my parents set with me is not an anomaly, nor is it the blueprint. Nonetheless, Black males in America are typically pushed, from birth, to be better than and to be nimble, disciplined and strong enough to remain sane and to live life in a society that considers them a problem. This negotiation, or orchestration as my mentor Professor Gordon likes to call it, is complex, nuanced and though not always socially acceptable is a success in its own right considering the perils of progressing as a Black male in the Western Hemisphere. These psychological successes are important to recognize. Therein lies the thinking behind this manuscript.

Too often scholarly research and popular culture present Black males within a faux orbit of one-dimensionality. There is the routine othering of Black males, the positioning of them outside a place of normalcy. As a rule, the way we understand Black males in American society is not in terms of success, at best it is in terms of survival. I argue here that within survival are abilities and attributes that mirror those found in the very best kind of successes. In operating from this perspective those abilities and attributes can inform identities that are psychologically stabilizing and socially rewarding. Most importantly, however, this text utilizes Black males as a tool in the push toward theory.

In growing up, as is stereotypic among many Black American males, I listened to a lot of hip-hop music—I still do. Within this genre I was always fascinated by the stories of racialized struggle and the negotiation of that struggle in the three to five minutes allotted for the record. It was tremendously motivational for me. Whether it be the incendiary rebellion of Ice Cube, Geto Boys and Public Enemy, the sophisticated articulation of KRS-One, De La Soul and Rakim, or the insightful social criticism of each, I was captivated by their storytelling and by the negotiated identities of these Black males amidst a reality of racial inequality and systematized oppression. Imagined or real, there was substantive psychological work being done that spoke to the agency and awareness of these Black males and to their ability to cope and to defy. I found messages here that extended beyond Black male rhyme writers.

In fashioning a dissertation idea I integrated this position on hip-hop music into personality psychology and my love of journalism. What came next was emphasis on identity via discourse, an appreciation of varying coping styles and of a universal human drive toward equilibrium. Still, the coping found in the Black male experience I saw as particularly salient and thought it a good illustration of how identities are driven toward stability. I have termed this very specialized stability Identity Stasis.

Identity Stasis is conceptualized as a psychological balance of identities and is introduced here as a theoretical and methodological framework, a few stops shy of formal theory. I advance Identity Stasis in this text through the prism of personality psychology, anchoring it in the identity construction of six Black American adolescent males through narratives and the technique of discourse analysis.

In looking at these young men and in looking at Identity Stasis there are fundamental assumptions from which I operate. I appreciate that the self is complex, that it provides a container for many identities, these identities are naturally driven toward a state of equilibrium and the identities avail themselves to an orchestrated balance that is person and situation driven.

This manuscript is not the nailing down of Identity Stasis as theory, rather a step forward that shows thinking to this point in time. from engaging Black male adolescents as cooperatives in defining who they are and in contributing to the deeper understanding of the whole of identity.

ACKNOWLEDGMENTS

Though an admittedly modest offering, there are many who have helped me to get this, my first work, out of the ether and onto paper. I thank God for breath and thought and will and love. I thank my wife Mikki. She is my best friend, the love of my life and most ardent support. And I thank my son Biko Harris Rice for being born to us. You are love and anchor your mother and me in all of the best things. My Mother is exceptional. I love her and I thank her for raising me with head and heart. I thank my Father and Grandmother for unconditional love. Thanks to Shebbie for making a path toward my first job and for helping me to get out of Howard on more than one occasion. Kris, you and Lance are my brothers, thank you both for being that. Thank you to my God Family—Beverly, Everod and Erin. Jean René, Shannon, Cassie, Chip and J.P., thank you for your very active support of my writing. Sekani, thank you for providing the soundtrack for this work. Coltrane, Max, Miles, Monk, Parker and Wynton thank you for being men. Georgette and Annie you are tremendous family and the best colleagues I'll ever have. Thank you to Jann H. Adams, your teachings while an undergraduate, your support as Department Chair and most of all your friendship mean more to me than you can imagine. Camara Jules P. Harrell you are the best of role models. A. Wade Boykin, thank you for sticking with me and for the introduction. Cynthia E. Winston, I thank you for your brilliance, patience and ever-present support and encouragement. I thank all of Howard University's Identity and Success Research Laboratory and appreciate the dedicated help and support of James Taliaferro and Rodney Terry. I also thank the Identity Stasis Lab—Patrick Bentley, Bryant Berry, William Marcel Hayes, Ian Harrell, Kareem Roberts, Carlton Lewis, Mark Starks, Jason Jones and Jacque-Corey Cormier. Thank you to the Morehouse College Department of Psychology. Jeanine, thank you for always making time for this project and for backing me from day one. Thank you to Aashir Nasim and to Kenneth Maurice Tyler, the constant conjunction. Thank you to the towering Intellects who cared enough to give a young thinker a kind word in delicately stepping toward your tremendous works: W. Curtis Banks, Reginald L. Jones, Asa G. Hilliard, III, Randall Robinson, William Cross III, Margaret Beale Spencer, Anderson J. Franklin, Howard C. Stevenson, James Jones, Lucius T. Outlaw, Jr., Robert M. Franklin, Jr., Walter E. Fluker, Michael Eric Dyson, Eddie S. Glaude, Jr., Robert Sellers, Tabbye Chavous, Nicole Shelton, Freeman A. Hrabowski, III and above all, the professor, Edmund W. Gordon, thank you for being such a beautiful person and for pushing me to be better.

INTRODUCTION

Contributions of Identity Stasis to Personality Psychology and Understanding the African American Male Lived Experience

Studying personality and the African American male lived experience is a daunting intellectual task. Scholars are faced with theoretical and methodological challenges in capturing the essence of the complexities of personality, while simultaneously integrating the cultural historical meaning of the intersections of race and gender. In this volume, Rice introduces a theoretical and methodological framework that assumes this challenge. Though a theory in its infancy, Rice's introduction of identity stasis is both timely and significant. There are several significant contributions that the theory of identity stasis makes to the field of personality psychology, as well as to increasing understanding about what it means to be an African American male in American society and culture.

With origins grounded in theoretical and methodological frameworks of race self complexity (see Winston et al., 2004; Winston, Philip and Lloyd, 2007; Terry and Winston, 2007), the theory of identity stasis makes two very significant theoretical and methodological contributions to the field of personality psychology. In terms of its theoretical contributions, identity stasis integrates recent contemporary personality theory with theory and research on the psychological meaning of race in novel ways to expand understanding of the lives of African American males. Identity stasis is among the very first personality theories in the field of psychology to use McAdams and Pals (2006) conceptualization of personality published in an article in the American Psychologist, *A New Big Five: Fundamental Principles for an Integrative Science of Personality*. These personality scholars challenge scholars of the person to conceptualize and study personality in ways that allow for description and explanation of human individuality situated in culture, social context and personhood. As such, they conceptualize personality as "an individual's unique variation on the general evolutionary design for human nature, expressed as a developing pattern of dispositional traits, characteristic adaptations and self defining life narratives, complexly and differentially situated in culture and social context" (McAdams and Pals, 2006, p. 204). This view of persons and personality opened new conceptual territory for the contributions of the study of the meaning of race within personality psychology. And identity stasis is on the cutting edge in traversing this uncharted conceptual terrain.

For example, within the field of personality psychology, there has been an under emphasis on studying the lives of African American males. As a result few personality theories take into account the unique complexities African American males' experience in negotiating internal and external stimuli in constructing an identity. The theory of identity stasis engages personality theory at both the characteristic adaptation and narrative identity levels of personality. Identity stasis is a personality process theory that includes the motives of the self system as an ego balancing mechanism and questions how achieving psychological equilibrium is accomplished in discursive acts of African American adolescent males. As such, these motives of the self become an overlapping part of the process of African American males' identity construction. This makes an important contribution not only to expanding understanding of the lives of African American males; it also can make a significant contribution to advancing knowledge of the self system through interrogating the complexities that the meaning of race adds to the self system of African American males.

Identity stasis introduces a new way to conceptualize the complexity of race within the identity development of African American adolescents who are at one of the most pivotal developmental periods in identity development. This analysis demonstrates how complicated identity construction can be for adolescents who are both in the infancy of the process of developing an internalized narrative of self related to race and also navigating the master narratives that are in society's public discourse about what it means to be an African American male adolescent.

The discourse of the six African American male adolescents who are used as instruments for understanding identity stasis confirms that the meaning of race in this society can create complicated personality development and psychological impositions. African American adolescents are negotiating all of the same developmental tasks associated with adolescence as their non-African American male peers, as well as having to define who they are as persons through psychologically balancing *"identity dilemma articulation," "unadulterated presentation of self"* and *"burden of proof assumption."* These psychological impositions become part of how adolescents manage race psychologically. African American male adolescents arguably experience the greatest amount of cultural racism in American society and therefore likely have the most complicated internal and external stimuli to negotiate as they construct their identity. This study's theoretical framework uniquely captures this psychological complexity.

The second significant contribution of identity stasis to personality psychology is aligned with the first but is more squarely focused on its methodological contributions. Less than a year after McAdams and Pals (2006) published their article, Robins, Fraley and Krueger published an edited research methods volume: Handbook of Research Methods in Personality Psychology (2007). As these authors note it is the very first of its kind in the history of personality psychology: the diversity of the research methods used by personality psychologists has not previously been represented in a single volume for researchers interested in conducting personality research. Personality scholars find themselves at a historical moment in which there is a significant emphasis on a diversity of personality research methods to explore new theoretical terrain to describe and explain the complexities of human life. Both of these developments highlight that it is a ripe time in the evolving intellectual story of an integrative science of personality to expand the methodological frameworks used to understand the meaning of race within the lives of African American males.

The theory of identity stasis is an example of personality theory driven methodological expansion within the field of personality psychology. For example, the integration of case study and discourse analytic research methods within the identity stasis strategy of inquiry extends the mission of personality psychology to the study of the lives of African American males. Though one of the historical missions of the field of personality psychology has been to understand human individuality through engaging study of the whole person, the field has largely fallen short in achieving this aim (McAdams and Pals, 2006). Within the field of personality psychology, the lives of African American males have not been the focus of theory development. Nor has their identity, a well-established core to personhood, been examined using strategies of inquiry and research methods that parallel the complexity of identity construction in the lived experience of African American males.

This methodological approach of studying African American males in terms of their lived experience of race compliments other well established methodological approaches to studying identity of African Americans. For example, Sellers and his colleagues (Sellers et al., 1997; 1998) have developed a multidimensional inventory of Black identity, which has been widely used to study the racial identity of African American males. What the discourse and case study strategy of inquiry used to study identity stasis does is elaborate on the contextual meaning and psychological function that some of the identity dimensions within Sellers model can take on in the process of African American males constructing their identity.

Similarly, Stevenson (2003) has studied African American male identity development and the complexities of the lived experience of African American males using a developmental ecological theoretical framework. Rice's use of discourse analysis coupled with a personality theoretical framework, complements the psycho- developmental approach of Stevenson and his colleagues.

The theoretical framework for this study converges with an important theoretical underpinning of the groundbreaking theory development and research on Nigrescence (Cross, 1991; Cross, Parham, and Helms, 1998). As a theory of identity development, Nigrescence, incorporates Black identity change as the core psychological aspect of the process of becoming Black. This theoretical perspective casts the individual on center stage as an agent of such change. Moreover, similar to the context in which African American males position what it means to be Black in their discourse, the identity change associated with the process of becoming Black occurs in the context of the master narratives about what it means to be Black at both the societal and local levels. In fact, it may be these master narratives that serve as a catalyst to stimulate the process of becoming Black to begin. The difference between agency in identity construction in discourse and the process of becoming Black is that in Nigrescence a person may have a more complicated combination of behavioral, emotional and cognitive challenges to integrate into his or her internalized and evolving narrative of self.

The methodological approach of employing discourse to advance understanding of identity stasis is aligned with Cross's identity theory of Nigrescence in very interesting ways as well. Both the theory of identity stasis and the theory of Nigrescence focus on agency as an important, complex and diverse part of a person's identity development. The distinction is that identity stasis focuses on the action in a person's identity construction in discourse, while Nigrescence theory centers on the action of identity change or metamorphosis within the context of a person's total sense of being and living. Discourse employed as a methodological tool of analysis and interpretation of psychological balance and complexity is novel not only in the study of the personality of African American males. This strategy of inquiry also makes a unique contribution to stimulating such a theoretical focus within the lives of all human persons. In essence, what the theory of identity stasis does is introduce an integrity based person centered strategy of inquiry, which both theoretically and methodologically allows for African American males to be studied as whole persons engaged in the complexities of identity construction.

In sum, identity stasis is a new personality theory that is timely and important. It is a theory that is born from a creative genius of engaging the complexities of the identity and lives of African American males, a group of human persons whom the field of personality psychology has largely neglected in its theoretical storehouse. The theoretical and methodological contributions of identity stasis to both the field of personality psychology and understanding human lives is occurring at a time when the meaning of race is increasing in its complexity within, what Jones (2003) describes as, the universal context of racism of American society and culture. It is also occurring at a time in which the field of personality psychology is intellectually ripe and fertile for new theoretical and methodological contributions to understand the complexity of human lives. This research significantly, with one study, expands the scholarly discourse on theoretical and methodological frameworks for studying the personality development of African American males in the twenty-first century.

Rice (2007) employs a complicated person centered analysis of the discourse of six African American males and grounds it in Du Boisan tenets of the psychological complexities of twoness to offer scholarly and practical insight into the lived experience of African American males. Indeed, this approach is not surprising given that this study of identity stasis was motivated by and born out of the intellectual genius of W. E. B. Du Bois. It was developed to tell a psychological and world story of its time, the past and the future. Du Bois's analysis of the world in which the Black man must traverse in the process of human development is a world of psychological complexities that evolve over time. These complexities are human ones. In emphasizing these psychological complexities, the theory of identity stasis gained its intellectual footing from the psychological and journalistic expertise of an early career scholar of his time—motivated to develop a theoretical and methodological mechanism to disseminate an integrative interpretative analysis of personality development.

Howard Thurman, a scholar and Dean of the Howard University Chapel, recognized that he had the power and access to create synergistic intellectual, spiritual and moral interactions among students, faculty and the wider community of Washington, DC, with his insights about human personality and lives. Rice's theory of identity stasis seeks a similar synergy and does so at a time when the stakes of not doing so for some can make the difference between psychological life and death. This intellectual boldness represents Rice's Howard University, Morehouse College and Edmund W. Gordon training and the intellectual roots of scholars who came before him challenging their own fields to take seriously the psychological complexities of the lives of African Americans in an American society and culture with a short-term memory.

Cynthia E. Winston, Ph.D.
Howard University and
The University of Michigan

ONE

Thinking toward Theory

The direction of present thinking was generated from drawings sketched some years ago in an effort make clear concepts that are often blurred within the social sciences—identity and the self. That group of illustrations morphed into a dissertation that had as core the Third Eye Model (TEM) of Race Self Complexity—now the Third Eye Model of Identity Negotiation. This model organized the self and affiliated identities around an expanding and contracting pupil that represented the psychological negotiating of cognitive stressors as formulated by Beaumiester (1999) in ego depletion and ego replenishment. TEM (figure 3.1) looked to explain adaptive selves and their relationship to external and internal stressors acknowledging cultural relativism through a lens of phenotypic variation in general and race self complexity specifically (Winston et al., 2004; Winston, Philip, and Lloyd, 2007; Terry and Winston, 2007). Initial ideas were and remain, to explore the complexity of identity through a construct that acknowledged reference group orientation, personal identity and the phenomena of individuation.

From TEM emerged a more complete representation of identity and self that employed psychological balance as fundamental. Again, a model was formulated to aid in clarity and the idea of identity stasis—balance—and identity static—imbalance resulted.

The Stasis/Static Model of Identity Negotiation (SMIN) is the scaffolding within which the Black male is considered in the present text. The model (figures 3.2–3.10) is an extension of W.E.B. Du Bois's (1897; 1903) double-consciousness, the Black American's negotiation of American and Black American identities. Within the Stasis/Static Model of Identity Negotiation the Black male's adapting proves a salient example of the work and goal of equilibrium as manifest in three forms of Identity Stasis: Identity Dilemma Articulation, Unadulterated Presentation of Self and Burden of Proof Assumption.

These components and building blocks of the Stasis/Static model are exemplars of bifurcated identity constructions that represent the awareness of identities to be negotiated, defiance in the face of negotiation and responsibility of identity assumption respectively. Through narratives provided by life story tellings, these forms of identity stasis provide arteries through which form and function of emerging selves are found. They also allow for more authentic approximations of Black male identity than those offered through rigid normative models that many times miss depth and scope of who individuals internalize and represent themselves to be.

Adaptation and Balance

Physiologist Walter Cannon developed the term homeostasis in explaining the fundamental property of complex systems to maintain stability (1932). Cannon further postulated homeostasis as not only a characteristic of endurance, but of adaptability to modifications of the environment (1939). This theory of equilibrium persists not only as a fundamental of physical sciences but also as rudimentary in the personality psychology activity of negotiating environments (Chess and Thomas, 1977; 1999; Freud, 1949; Jung, 1921; Erikson, 1968; Maslow, 1968). In considering homeostasis an essential characteristic of all living organisms, this exploratory analysis attends to the balance of internal and external psychological circumstances as a natural process toward identity and a goal of identity stasis. We get to this balance through self.

The constellation of self-systems provides a tapestry by which identity theorists illustrate the active striving for psychological balance. Identity, the self, self-concept and self-aspects, then, are presented here as the instruments by which a person is able to coordinate behavior that is adapted to both internal and external stimuli in an effort to achieve equilibrium.

Identity, Self and Self-Concept

Identity is frequently confused because of the amorphous nature of the construct and an inability of social scientists to settle on universal meaning. In this exercise of pushing theory forward, identity is understood as a peculiar quality or flavoring (Erikson, 1963; McAdams, 2003) of self-understanding through arrangement and configuration. To the extent that a person's self-understanding is integrated synchronically and diachronically such that it situates him or her in a meaningful psychological niche and provides his or her life with some degree of unity or purpose, that person "has" identity (McAdams, 2001).

Within this writing identity is considered an active agent of the self, allowing the self-system to operate as a coherent whole relative to circumstance (Baumeister, 1986; Markus and Wurf, 1987). McAdams (1999; 2001; 2003) brings clarity to this conceptualization in his life story theory of identity and Appiah (2004) extends this idea with the assertion that "to adopt an identity, to make it mine, is to see it as structuring my way through life. That is, my identity has patterns built into it, patterns that help me to think about my life." Indeed, this "thinking about" or perhaps thinking through, or thinking toward is the essence of identity and positions the individual within a relationship of best fit.

Chess and Thomas (1977; 1999) use the term goodness of fit in matching the environment and its expectations to the individual's abilities in a psychologically healthy situation. This clinical approach complements the thinking here and helps in the consideration of contours within the developmental arc. Goodness of fit allows for a substantive jumping-off point toward focused attending to identity.

No doubt the positioning of identity is complex. Though narratives are utilized here to give form to identity, there remains the psychosocial, cultural and intrapsychic domains that Sedekedies and Brewer (2001) explain through representations of individual, relational and collective selves. These selves are self-concept iterations that further layer identity and prove key in fully considering the construct.

The self-concept is a cognitive generalization about the self that contains traits, values and episodic and semantic memories that organize and guide the processing of self-related information (Campbell et al., 1996; Kihlstrom and Cantor, 1984; Markus, 1977). The self-concept also demonstrates the complexity of the self and identity through self-aspects, non-redundant selves (Linville, 1985; 1987) that represent pieces to the jigsaw puzzle of the self. Self-complexity is also thought of here in terms of authenticity of self-aspects and their able integration (Ryan et al., 2005) into a complete self.

In working toward an integrated understanding of identity and the self structure, identity stasis is theorized as the self's orchestration of self aspects into cooperative balance.

Identity Stasis

Identity stasis is presented as a theoretical construct of pursued psychological balance within personality psychology. The psycho-sociological framework is informed by a theory driven and inclusive approach to diverse human functioning (Spencer, 2004). Identity stasis concerns itself with the whole person considering context. The present thinking supports the understanding of identity stasis by emphasizing the categorical variables of race and gender intending to explore the two looking beyond typical gap outcomes that are frequently tethered to analysis of the subaltern cultures of Black males (Gordon, 2005).

Identity is understood in this text as self-understanding through arrangement and configuration of the self relative to circumstance via life story. Accordingly, identity stasis is presented as an individual's orchestration of multiple identities to circumstance in the effort to achieve equilibrium.

Instantiations of identity stasis found in the data used suggest the theoretical framework as a process. The process is rooted in McAdams and Pals' (2006) New Big Five mapping. Again, identity stasis is situated in personality psychology and has as its thrust a consideration of identities and their impact on the whole person. In accord with this emphasis, the process of identity stasis is activity that is defined by the personality principles of characteristic adaptation, life narratives and the challenge of modern identity and the differential role of culture. These three principles are evident in an analysis of our participants' movement toward psychological balance through identity construction by way of identity dilemma articulation, unadulterated presentation of self and burden of proof assumption; the three forms of identity stasis tagged in support of the developing theoretical and methodological framework.

The data in this manuscript has allowed for a maturing of the initial forms of identity stasis outlined above and has also demonstrated a very specific type of identity stasis activity that attends to race and gender. At once situated in a self and identity domain, the identity stasis characteristic of these young Black males' activity represents negotiated integration of racial identification into other self-identities. Their particular identity stasis is further understood as the end point, however temporary, at which the integration is achieved. This activity and endpoint casts identity stasis as both a process and a state. Notable is that in negotiating equilibrium there is not a proposed dichotomy of identification, rather a palette of identities available to orchestration in whatever way the individual determines most psychologically appropriate.

The "specialized" stasis that the data set exhibited is both a strand of the larger design of identity stasis and a peculiar cultural node that probes in a way that allows the complexity of identity construction associated with race to be adapted into the identity and self whole. Important to note is that with respect to racial identity, Cross (1991) is interwoven into our general backdrop, staking identity as a social and socialized construct that carries the weight of interactions in the formation of identity and individuation. For example, here it is concluded that for Black Americans, identity stasis is, in significant part, manifest as a psychological adaptation to the dilemma of double-consciousness (Du Bois, 1897). While double-consciousness is the psyche's struggle between the Black cultural and American identities, identity stasis looks to thread "warring ideals" through a singular eye of self, integrating disparate aspects into a complex working whole.

Again, the process of identity stasis is exhibited here in participant life stories as analyzed through discourse analysis. Support for the identity stasis construct is indicated in identity negotiation through identity dilemma articulation, burden of proof assumption and unadulterated presentation of self.

The process extends toward balance-as-goal as the individual is able to cope with racialized contexts in a way that allows them to operate beyond, over or through such that cognitive energies remain relatively untaxed.

Stasis and Static

Identity stasis, particularly among Black males, has demonstrated not only a representation of adaptation, but also suggests reconsiderations of adapting. Notable among these re-thinkings are issues of coping, defiance, ego-control and ego depletion/replenishment (Baumiester, 2001).

The Stasis/Static Model of Identity Negotiation was developed in order to cleanly consider these concepts. The model (figures 3.2–3.10) is a conceptual graphic linking Identity stasis with cognitive and emotional functioning toward balance. The model helps to clarify identity stasis by relationships and further speaks to the utility of engaging the subject and the particular utility of considering Black males beyond stereotype noting that they prove a salient sample able to give better structure and substance to these particular psycho-social phenomena.

The Stasis/Static Model attends to contexts and the adaptability of identity to internal and external stimuli and stressors. This coping is in turn dependent on how each context is integrated into identity behavior. The process of identity stasis is achieved when the context is negotiated in such a way as to render stimuli and stressors of that context manageable, considered and integrated to a point where cognitive energies are able to be focused elsewhere. Identity stasis finds root in the balance that each self aspect strikes with another. It is postulated that other salient cultural and situational devices of identity add to a foundational self-intricacy and must also find balance space.

Alternatively, identity static occurs when contextual stimuli and stressors impact to a point where the individual is cognitively compromised relative to identity negotiation. Results of this tax do not necessarily shred identities, however, they can contribute to their incompleteness with cognitive energies being focused in areas that do not allow for the full potential of the identities.

For example, identity static could be found in an individual who is highly engaged in academics. While the context of the academy does not determine one's identity, the adaptation to environment could cause an internal preoccupation with an academic self that eclipses the fullness of other selves/identities. This ego depletion (Baumeister, 1998; 1999; 2001) does not have to persist, however. With familiarity to the context and lessened sensitivity, the associated stressors/stimuli allow for ego replenishment and stasis in the self/identity of concern.

The Stasis/Static Model relative to Black males is looked at through a lens that considers a self concept that is complicated by the biopsychological and cultural historical tenants of race self complexity (Winston et al., 2004; Terry and Winston, 2007). Accordingly, it is posited that balance occurs for Black people within the United States through an Identity stasis that is informed by specialized psychological racial work.

Existentialism and Personality

By utilizing existentialism in the present theoretical and methodological framework there is not the want to place the understanding of identity or of the Black male into the distant philosophical, quite the opposite. Existentialism a research orientation looks to come closer to the full understanding of identity through the Black male by partnering with the "studied" in understanding.

Approaching identity through the Black male and the sphere of existentialism is done by differentiating between the explanation of the nature of being

Black (Baldwin and Wright) and a description of the Black male experience (Du Bois and Ellison) while utilizing both perspectives to triangulate in understanding meaning and purpose of Black identification. The balance of this Black identity with other identities—identity stasis—helps to integrate the nature and meaning of being Black without isolating them or relegating them as mutually exclusive. It is anticipated, then, that this very specific identity would give understanding to other identities in terms of form, function, nature and beyond.

Focus on the meaning and purpose of this Black identity balance also connects with a primary utility of stressing a personality psychology that attends to meaning as does the construction of identity through life story tellings (Erikson 1968; Jones, 2005; Winston, 2004; 2005; McAdams, 2004).

As discussed in the preface and in points throughout this book, literature on Black males (scholarly and otherwise) places heavy emphasis on him as deficient. This is the rule rather than the exception. And this rule is weak when placed under the critical eye of rational and empirical thought. The assumption of "less than all of the time" is flawed in both approach and in epistemological, axiological and ontological assumptions. Existentialism and a positive view of human potential are used here in reconsidering the Black male as a "whole person" allowing for personality psychology to serve in further grounding identity stasis.

In addition to the New Big Five (McAdams and Pals, 2006), here personality is appreciated as the set of psychological traits and mechanisms within the Black male that are organized, are relatively enduring and that influence his interactions with and adaptations to the environment (Larsen and Buss, 2002). Again, the whole person is of particular attention in personality psychology and the characteristics (traits) and activities (mechanisms) that an individual organizes within develop the identity and help that identity to balance external and intrapsychic phenomena (environments). A person-centered approach that looks to the Black male for partnership in identity construction and definition is bounded in the existential and in personality because of an acknowledgement of the sum total of the individual.

Black Male Culture and Cultural Relevance by Example

Cross (2006, personal conversation) discusses a blur in analysis that compares race and ethnicity suggesting culture as more defining and of greater relevance. Appiah (2005) extends this argument of overlapping constructs in his assertion that to focus on cultural identity (i.e., differences) misses the point largely because of the natural variation of individuals. In approaching both issues there is the ability to be theory generative rather than oppositional. This allows for multiple perspectives that get lost in validating the/a "Black" perspective. Accordingly, there is the need and opportunity to deal with conceptual differences and why these differences are ripe for consideration.

For example, in addressing "deepening plight of Black males," one must consider the oft-tossed term "success" relative to circumstance. With the illustration of the Black male as "disconnected" there is almost always the situating of him in a context of dire straits, far, far away from education. If, however, there are narrow circumstances or contexts within which academic opportunities lead to success (the typically assumed predictor of connectedness and social norm), this path is side-stepped in favor of alternatives that are demonstrated, modeled and that appear accessible and feasible to the individual. A perspective of defiance, resilience and adaptability are seen here in that there is the negotiating of self to fit within dictated contexts or circumstances. There is adaptation and advance that may not be in line with "normed" cultural mores, but that fit the individual's context. There is success here where measures of success are considered on very basic levels. Maslow (1943) conceived these levels in terms of needs. Deficiency needs (physiological, safety, love/belonging, status) are the most basic and are innovatively achieved despite situations that suggest failure for many Black males. In a poverty-ravaged community, for instance, community with little infrastructure and compromised governmental and social support, success might be defined as surviving and in securing spots of happiness. This may or may not come in the form of academic rigor and/or responsibilities that tend to attach themselves to Maslow's higher-level being needs (self-actualization, self-transcendence).

So, if we know that there are successes of different types considering circumstance and that culture, context and cultural context will often times define types of success and resilience and adaptability, then we see that it is important to consider difference–cultural, socio-economic, biopsychological, cultural historical and others. For those who are "disconnected," "at the lower quartile" and whatever other traditionally deficit language we might attribute, we must consider the success that they have achieved—that is they are alive despite, are raising a family despite, are in school despite, or in college despite.

In taking these successes into account we have an opportunity to not so much look at resilience, but at defiance—the ability to succeed as a motivational response to or because of. And there is also the opportunity to look at the traditionally successful and their patterns. There are multiple streams of self definition and success available to consideration. And each success, that of the upper and ordinary achiever, reasons for each circumstance and how to pull all of these situations together in an effort to improve and to provide models that are appropriate for replication are important activities.

Adolescence and Narratives

A sample of Black male adolescents was used in this grounded thinking to examine affirmative development. Approaching through this formative, frank and pivotal stage of maturation without the dire film of hopelessness allows for perspective beyond stereotype.

Narrative theories of personality explain that as individuals approach adolescence, they create internalized narratives. The narrative serves as a means of internal sight, an autobiographical identity that is able to make sense of external stimuli in terms of evaluation, categorization and subsidization and has the capacity to offer a continuity with past experiences, commentary on current concerns and a template for future actions (Singer, 1995).

Accordingly, to focus on Black males during adolescence gives unique insight into formation, expression and self-definition that frames potential and that suggests forms of continued growth through linguistic expression and life story tellings. With respect to the larger Black male corpus, focus here allows for a trajectory of development that can be bolstered or, if necessary, augmented toward more healthy identification and behavior.

Stevenson (2003) further contends in his addressing Black males that, "in the mind of the adolescent, doing rather than being may best represent the identity striving. This becoming occurs in abstract and across time, but most youth are being or doing, not solely becoming." This contending in reference to Black males addresses imperatives that are frequently discounted, 1) that Black males are developing and evolve beyond the discreet phase of adolescence and 2) that activity, in this instance through talk, is particularly important to explore as an adolescent strives/copes toward identity (Spencer, 1999; Youngblood and Spencer, 2002).

The Black Male Adolescent

In advancing identity stasis as a theoretical concept there is an opportunity to consider the Black male beyond the typically expected and expressed. Psychological research concerning Black males routinely addresses what is wrong with them. This is not dissimilar from traditional psychological and social psychological research that trends toward psychological functions of the negative and attends to distortions and/or flaws within individuals (Wetherell and Potter, 1992). The deficit model and its relation to the Black male, however, presents as particularly acute.

Many studies hold to the forefront statistics that help to objectify and distance one from the subject of the Black male, but there is rarely inquiry into who Black males are beyond self shells that are constructed within and presented to mass culture.

Alternatively, by utilizing Black males and their uniquely specialized status and development within the United States, there is the ability to succinctly advance the understanding and viability of identity stasis while also approaching research concerning this often misrepresented sample by employing methodology that engages the individual. Here this is done with a special focus on the Black male adolescent. This developmental phase allows for the activity of negotiation and adaptation to appear as particularly salient providing a powerful dynamic within which to consider identity stasis. Approaching Black male adolescents from a normal perspective that assumes a fundamental fit with others despite, but cognizant of individual differences is where identity stasis and the Black male intersect—the analysis of one allows for a better understanding of the other while also filling in research gaps resulting from the positioning of Black male adolescents as less or other than.

Despite negatively skewed published research and popular media concerning Black male adolescents, most would accept that this specialized sample is complex and multidimensional. In stepping toward this sophisticated identity it is helpful to consider the voice of the subject. Doing so gives a nuanced understanding of human behavior that allows for greater insight on micro and macro levels.

Engagement and meaning making here, again, comes in the form of narratives representing negotiated identities. Looking at the perspectives, words and text of six adolescent Black males demonstrated the activity of managing bifurcated identities as paramount in the articulation of self concept.

These findings, though not representative in a classic sense, suggest the importance of pursuing a measured consideration of identity and self. This fresh-eyed perspective allows the concept of identity stasis space within a web of complimentary constructs that begins with double-consciousness.

Double-Consciousness, Toward and Beyond

> The double consciousness referred to by Du Bois was the dual status of being both American and Black. We further recognize the quandary of being American, Black and male. In America, stereotypical male behavior takes on a different meaning when related to Black males. Behavior which may be evaluated as daring, independent-minded, or exciting when seen in majority culture (i.e., European American) males, may be seen as dangerous or threatening in Black males. Similar behavior takes on different meaning (Spencer et al., 1997).

One hundred and ten years after the introduction of double-consciousness, Black American adolescent males live and must develop a sense of who they are in a world more sophisticated than the one Du Bois described. There is the appearance of Black culture contributions in mass culturally themed mores (music, athletics, comedy, acting, etc.). However, the duality of "fitting in" is further complicated in having to determine an authentic fit or nonfit with suggested culture contributions that are frequently misaligned with identity. This spun culture is often bound in a Manichean psychology (Fanon, 1967; Harrell, 1999). A psychology of dualistic contrast between individual and other that positions the minds of many Black people in a space that is so situated in the context of racialized polarity that there is special importance attributed to intrapsychic balance.

Accordingly, though the stability scenario that Du Bois put forth in 1897 remains foundational in the complex self-construction for Blacks, there are additional dimensions that require the push of theory and method in an effort to fully capture a fundamental duality inherent in a Black life and connected quandaries (Boykin, 1986).

Interpretational Analysis and Context

Steps toward this engaged approach and pushes forward are found in an interpretational emphasis. Gordon (1991) talks of interpretational analysis within the sciences as a path of sorts that sees a continuum from experimental, through correlational to interpretation. Psychology has the analysis as extending from Cronbach's (1957) steady stressing of experimental and correlational strategies to Lewin's (1946) base of individual and environment interaction.

From Lewin's context dependent epistemological foundation others helped to further shape this often neglected interpretive lens of human behavior. Dollard (1935) contended that the understanding of behavior could not be reasonably considered absent context. Murray (1938) delineated that physical and internally motivated responses to the physical (alpha and beta environments respectively) were necessary in considering human events. And Pettigrew (1968) contended a cyclical compliment between quantitative and qualitative inquiry, emphasizing the need for both in order to approach fuller understanding of human behavior.

Nonetheless, an a contextual approach to the research of human behavior often prevails to the detriment of an authentic human understanding. Context is frequently ignored by a science that is somewhat obsessively conscious of prediction and control because of the loose ends that often result in having to deal with circumstance and the essence of being an individual. Sternberg and Grigorenko (2004) aptly explain:

> A contextual research is . . . highly rewarded because it is usually experimentally more elegant than the mess we confront when we attempt to study children in their natural and diverse sociocultural contexts and easier to interpret, even if the interpretation is limited to some imaginary microworld in which children do not really live.

The a contextual approach appears as stingingly detrimental to the full understanding of Black (adolescent) males because there is an incomplete scope of the individual, only clips of narrow experiences piled upon one another. The result is a singular image of the Black male draped in a tangled pathology (Reed, 2003) documented by the academy, reinforced by the media and acted on by society. In relation to Black males, then, beyond the quantitative, there becomes a necessitated question of context. What is the field within which Black males are interacting and, further, defining themselves?

Field Theory and Agency

In reemphasizing the importance of context, field theory must be appreciated (Lewin, 1946), a theory that suggests that context matters and the fact that it matters is of crucial significance because of the consequences that abound as the result of its functioning. The context, or field of interest, is comprised of culture, personality, interpersonal and intergroup relationships extending from the past into the future and this context exists as an individual's perspective at any given time (Jones, 2003). With this understanding it can be said that context is a constant that individuals must negotiate in their daily psychological functioning.

This sensibility is also informed by Black identity pioneer William Cross' (1991) recasting of the Horowitzes two-factor model of Black identity. In slightly tweaking group identity into reference group orientation, Cross puts forward a reconsidered two-factor model in which there is greater significance attributed to the individual relative to group, that is in turn dependent on social positioning, social context or social field.

An overarching social field that Blacks must negotiate is buoyed by racial difference. This is not to suggest that race is definitive of any particular behavior. Certainly, Blacks are not posited as Universal Turing machines operating in a strict connectionist paradigm. Approaching from a social cognitive perspective, there is agency, consciousness and identity (Bandura, 1999; 2001)—with race interwoven. The degree to which race is a factor is dependent on how the individual responds to phenotypic variation within a triadic (internal personal factors, behavioral patterns and environmental events) causation interplay that is dependent on the activities, situational circumstances and sociostructural constraints and opportunities afforded (Bandura, 1986; 1999; 2001).

Racism as Context

Irrespective of how, race plays big in this triadic causation interplay for Blacks, primarily because of racism. Racism is a perceived psychological context for Blacks because of their operating within a universal context of racism (Jones, 2003). Racism is defined as a presupposition of one's own racial group over another and rationalizes privileged dominance (Harrell, 1999; Jones, 2003). It is manifest on three very distinct and permeating levels. Individual racism occurs in the activity of racial prejudice, institutional racism finds root in organizational practice and policy and cultural racism exists in the form of values, beliefs, symbols and myths (Harrell, 1999).

A universal context of racism, then, gives Blacks a cultural historical perspective (Vygotsky, 1978; Winston et al., 2004) from which to construct a personal and collective past, present and future self (Jones, 2003). Consequently, racism as a context informs this construction and the construction is frequently predicated on oppression and disenfranchisement via individual, institutional and cultural avenues. This context also gives rise to two primary, taxing motivations: self-protective from racism and self-enhancing one's worth and humanity. Therefore, a universal context of racism can be understood as a psychological reality at any given time for Blacks having the capacity to influence behavior by way of motivation and functioning.

To understand the act—the behavior—one has to understand its socio-cultural elements. Each act reflects such elements as well as impacts on them. With respect to youth development Spencer (2006) often refers to this as the bi-directionality of behavior and environment. Things never remain constant; they are constantly changing. Human actions are dynamically and dialectically related to their context. One act influences subsequent acts. So goes the process, much in the same way as proprioceptive processes where a response in one part of an organism stimulates a different response in another part of the organism producing feedback and change.

The Activity of Engagement

In pressing the theoretical and methodological framework of identity stasis and in an attempt to look at avenues toward substantiation, a case study approach was employed. Like many case studies conducted within personality psychology, multiple strategies of inquiry were included in order to elicit full engagement of the participants. These strategies were informed by several theoretical orientations as outlined in the following chapters.

Discursive analysis of data segments drawn from focus groups demonstrate identity stasis as represented in (1) Identity Dilemma Articulation, (2) an Unadulterated Presentation of Self and in (3) Burden of Proof Assumption. In this text the conceptual grounding and implications of these three forms of identity stasis for advancing identity theory are discussed, as are the possible psychological functions that identity stasis may serve in personality development and expression.

Two

Underpinnings

One ever feels his two-ness—an American, a Negro; two souls, two thoughts, two warring ideals in one dark body, whose dogged strength alone keeps it from being torn asunder.

W. E. B. Du Bois (1903)

That kind of makes it hard for me to, like, know who I am. 'Cause if I am putting on a front for white people and then I act a certain way when I am with other people, it's like, who does that make me?

Coltrane (2003)

The individual is engaged so that we can better understand and appreciate the sophistication of the whole person. This is the existential orientation that is used to go beyond typical research involving Black males and identity. Often social scientists are quick to discount the uniqueness of the human condition in an obsession with boxing behavior. Absolute is the resulting misplaced objective rather than approximations that help to further individual understanding. Where the core tendency of personality in existential psychology is to achieve authentic being (Maddi, 1996), here we look to find that authenticity looking at the courage and hardiness points in adolescence that situate an ideal of individuality.

This analysis is commentary supported by data that extends beyond the classic experimental toward theoretical and methodological approaches when looking at human identification. In accord with this perspective our exercise is in developing theory and method advances related to how identity integration—defined as identity stasis—is represented in the identity construction of Black adolescent males. There is also an effort to incorporate into this theory and method development an understanding of what this integration means.

These goals are advanced through outline, the staking of the individual relative to context and previous theory. The underpinnings of identity stasis are primarily informed by McAdams and Pals's (2006) New Big Five, Du Bois's (1897; 1903) Black identity as informed by double-consciousness, Freud's (1949) id, ego and superego and Jones's (1991) politics of personality with other theories providing texture to these broad strokes.

Personality

Traits are a collective of relatively enduring behaviors that govern how individuals negotiate their physical, psychic and intrapsychic environment (Allport, 1954; Jones, 1991; Larsen and Buss, 2002; Kambon, 1992). The mainline of psychology has taken traits and made them synonymous with personality. Jung extended Freud with focus on temperaments, Eysenck approached from a factor analytic orientation to substantiate dimensions of personality and McCrae and Costa (1994) refined Eysenck with the five-factor model of personality based on extroversion, neuroticism, conscientiousness, agreeableness and openness to experience. The Big Five, as it is often called, provides reliable shorthand to the individual, this substantiated by its stature within psychology and beyond given the respectability of the NEO-Personality Inventory.

Nonetheless, traits alone do not reflect present thinking on personality. McAdams and Pals (2006) provide the integrative approach to personality within which identity stasis fits. While respecting the baseline of trait theory and its outline of personality, the New Big Five suggests the incorporation of principles that take into account personality psychology fundamentals, specifically the analysis of the whole person from a perspective that attends to how the individual person is like all other persons, how the individual person is like some other persons and how the individual person is like no other person (Kluckhohn and Murray 1953; McAdams and Pals 2006).

The principles that direct this approach to personality are imbedded in the way in which individuals vary in evolutionary design and the expression of that variation through dispositional traits. There is also an attending to the uniqueness of the individual through characteristic adaptation, or contextualized motivational, social-cognitive and developmental adaptations. Identity through purposeful, unitary life stories that bring cohesion to one within the world and the differential role of culture are the final two principles that establish the orientation of this analytic exercise.

This perspective provides a vocabulary by which to consider the form and function of identity stasis within a life. It formalizes the, at once, independent and unitary nature of personality and suggests that Black males, by definition, benefit from "an integrative science of personality." Accordingly, the phenotypic variation of our sample, their gender and the context of the United States are suggestive of relatively unique dispositional traits. The differential role of culture on personality could allow for a particularly rich understanding of identity stasis through characteristic adaptation and in valuing life story narratives as a unitary function of personality. Its understanding through discourse analysis should yield meaningful data that informs the five principles.

Essentially, the uniqueness of Black American males, identity stasis and the New Big Five help to press toward an understanding of negotiated, bifurcated identities relative to other identities and the self. The termed bifurcation, of course, is an extension of Du Boisian thought.

Double-consciousness

Black identity has been widely researched within the discipline of psychology, but none have offered greater contribution in making plain the complexities of Black identification than sociologist W. E. B. Du Bois (1897; 1903). His philosophical fit with respect to identity stasis lies most squarely in his conceptualization of double-consciousness. With double-consciousness Du Bois explains an inherently spliced identity of the Black American where there exists a Black social experience governed by core norms, mores and socialized expectations and a dominant society experience with different and frequently inconsistent norms, mores and socialized expectations that must be integrated into the identity and behavior of Black people.

The cultural historical perspective of race (Vygotsky, 1978; Winston et al., 2004; Winston, Philip, and Lloyd, 2007; Terry and Winston, 2007) that Du Bois highlights in the necessity to "be both a Negro and an American, without being cursed and spit . . . to be a coworker in the kingdom of culture" is a phenomena that the Black American is consistently driven to reconcile. It is a relentless psychological activity.

Very much in-line with Du Bois's thinking, this analysis positions double-consciousness as the negotiation of two psychological realities that are defined by Black cultural and American norms that are race-specific and that are often in diametric contrast (Boykin, 1986; 1995). Among the Black males participating in our analysis, identity stasis is demonstrated as a psychological representation of double-consciousness and as part of the larger identity's effort toward balance.

For these Black male adolescents identity stasis is specialized by race because of its salience, but is not defined by it. Their balance is universal in that it is a unique orchestration of identities in an effort to manifest one pivotal self-concept within a layer/lens of the self system. Their particular stasis operates within a universal context of racism (Jones, 2004) in an attempt to achieve a relatively stable unified identity (Rice, 2004). And though there may not be a full awareness of the process of their identity stasis, the integration of a Black identity–to whatever extent–into the self-system is indication that the construct is present and has activity.

The Triple Quandary (Boykin, 1986) is a psychological extension of double-consciousness. The theoretical framework proposes social realms within which the Black American transacts in achieving a Black identity (Boykin, 1986; Boykin and Ellison, 1995). There is Du Boisian double-consciousness's mainstream and Black culture experience, and a minority realm that delineates a shared experience with non-whites around areas of oppression and marginalization. Boykin (1986; 1995) matures the Du Boisian Black cultural by emphasizing an African cultural ethos and interrelated dimensions of spirituality, harmony, movement, verve, affect, communalism, expressive individualism, oral tradition and social time perspective. The extent to which there is participation or orientation to the social realms defines the Black identity assumed and the multiplicity of the Triple Quandary. Understanding double-consciousness as informed by social experiences that the Triple Quandary affords is cornerstone in the developing mold of identity stasis. There is also Boykin's appreciation of the complexity of those experiences, the Afrographic nature of their analysis and an emphasis on Black American youth that influence this work.

The Manichean psychology (Fanon, 1967; Harrell, 1999) of white as good and Black as bad is another perspective through which identity stasis is considered for these young Black males. The very complex nature of the racism that presents itself helps in determining the function of identity stasis. Identity as coping is substantiated where Harrell (1999) marks a Manichean framed violence, a violation of the social and psychological integrity of the group or individual (Bulhan, 1985; Harrell, 1999). This type of violence (among others) is regularly visited on young Black males, again supporting a focus on this sample in exploring the salient dynamics of identity stasis.

Manichaean psychology, the Triple Quandary and Du Bois's double-consciousness provide an invaluable intersection of theory that aids in the understanding of Black identity and self-complexity. In fashioning identity stasis these conceptualizations contribute to the theoretical and methodological understanding of the individual's pursued psychological balance.

The Black identification that these young males achieve is pivotal in how they progress psychologically because of the coping patterns and behaviors that result from this identification, persistence of these patterns and the patterns influence on other behaviors beyond those directly related to race.

Race, Being Black

Though racial identity with respect to Black Americans has been heavily researched with remarkable steps made toward understanding what it means to be identified as Black or to assume a Black identity (Cross, 1971; Sellers, 1997, 98; Triandis, 1988, 89; Markus and Wurf 1987; Campbell, 1990, 96; Phinney, 1990; Parham and Helmes, 1985; Oyersman, 1995), there remains room for refinement and reconsideration. Within proposed theoretical frameworks, theories and suggestions, lines are frequently blurred between alternate definitions of identity and personal fallacies and fantasies about what it means to identify as being Black, making conclusions based on "Blackness" difficult and inconsistent.

In the United States Black identity is commonly accepted as the extent to which one operates within the socio-cultural assignment of being descendant of a displaced race; the product of slaves who were brought to the Americas from varied regions of Africa and who exist today cloaked in a legacy of dehumanization, oppression and marginalization (Cross, 1996; Kambon, 1992). And then there are Black Americans who find their way to the United States absent the compromising influence of slavery; cultural legacy in tact, but still assumed and engaged as marginalized within the social order. Though the depth of the Black American experience extends beyond the dictates of a racialized environment, race remains a factor. Consequently, the approach that psychologists take in addressing race is of critical importance in examining Black identity.

Race is a social construct that partitions along the lines of ethnically dictated physical appearance. There is no biological basis for race, however, there are deep and enduring behaviors that are manifest along the social partitions of the construct (Feagin and Feagin, 1996; Jones, 1997). Real or not, race has definite psychological actions, consequences and reactions for Black Americans and as a result of its categorizing dynamics, there develops a variety of racial groups that are segmented into socially dominant (white) and marginalized (other). Activities that occur as a result of this categorizing are necessary to consider in the comprehensive analysis of the psychology and identity of Black people. The three domains of cognitive activity influenced within the targets of racism are the formation of beliefs about the efficacy and competence of human beings as a function of their race, the influence on standards of beauty and body image and the accurate assessment of history and culture (Harrell, 1999). The levels on which racism operate are complete—individual, institutional and cultural (Jones, 1997). Still, there are selves beyond those responding to racism that speak directly to the complexity of identity and self-definition.

Cutting-edge scholars have written in terms of Double-consciousness (Du Bois, 1903), a Triple Quandary (Boykin, 1986), Manichean Psychology (Fanon, 1967; Harrell, 1999), the Invisibility Syndrome (Franklin, 2004), Nigrescence (Cross, 1991) and other innovative thinking, but their overtures to Black identity are too often ignored within the greater scope of identity research. Therefore, exploring the intricacies of race within the larger question of identity with their work as base allows for significant advances in understanding the whole of the self system through the identity construction of the Black American adolescent male.

The intent of this quilting of ideas is to generate themes concerning Black identity that integrate fundamental aspects of identity and self in attempting to understand identity stasis. The special emphasis on identity stasis also looks to self-complexity (Linville, 1985; 1987; Rafaeli-Mor, 2002), identity construction and the dimensionality/self-complexity interplay.

Chapter Two

Black Identity and Identity Stasis

Understanding Black identity is limited by considering it in an isolated context, absent fundamental, broad theory. This circumscribed view allows for the misinterpretation of behaviors and stifles a deeper understanding of the significance of race in the everyday living of Black people. Consequently, there is an opportunity to consider Black identity within the larger pool of self and identity research in order to achieve a more complete analysis that integrates the importance of race into an understanding of self and identity relative to Black people. The present analysis looks at Black identity from this perspective in an effort to link it with identity stasis and dynamics associated with the self in order to advance understanding concerning the whole of identity.

Foundational theories of identity have consistently challenged researchers within the discipline of psychology to innovate in their attempts to explain the self. Descartes' (1641) "I think therefore I am," illustrates the desire of human beings to comprehend their conceptual and behavioral inner-workings and the want to distinguish between the "I" and the "me" (James, 1890) pushes theories of identity to move beyond immediate perceptual understandings of self definitions. An important other step in the development of identity lies in an integrated consideration of the significance of race and culture.

In exploring identity theory and psychology in general, norms are commonly understood within the context of a white male template assumed to be applicable to and appropriate for all (Azibo, 1986; Boykin, 1986; Bynum, 1999; Harrell, 1999; Akbar, 2004), incidentally considering issues of race and culture. Alternatively, theories that address marginalized individuals and groups often make impactful contributions but fail to incorporate broad psychology or social theory that is relevant, becoming isolated and missing opportunities to place general identity theory at higher levels. With identity stasis there is a theoretical and methodological perspective consistent with Black culture and inclusive of fundamental identity queries, allowing for substantive reconsideration of Black identity and identity theory.

This analysis positions identity within the social psychological as an active agent of the self. It is a mechanism that functions such that the self-system is a coherent whole, a phenomenon that shares space within the self-concept and requires energy to maintain equilibrium (Baumeister, 1986; Markus and Wurf 1987). Identity stasis functions such that identities within the self and the psychological process of self-construction that individuals are called upon to achieve (McAdams, 1999; 2001) remain balanced. This activity toward balance is evident in Black identification because of the bifurcated nature of the Black person's lived experience.

Identity is effectively understood through the self-concept, which is defined in contemporary research as a cognitive schema. Schemas are cognitive generalizations that contain traits, values, episodic and semantic memories about the self and organize and guide the processing of self-related information (Campbell, et al. 1996; Kihlstrom and Cantor, 1984; Markus, 1977). Identity schemas are types of cognitive structures that serve as cognitive bases for arriving at definitions of situations in which persons find themselves (Stryker and Serpe, 1994).

The self-concept is key in the development of identity. It is a core that informs the action and reaction of related mechanisms in the self system, proving a significant part of the self constellation. The Black males in this analysis hold Black identity as relevant to their self-concept. As a result, other aspects of the self are impacted with its assumption and can be best understood against the backdrop self-complexity.

Linville (1985; 1987) explains self-complexity as the number of non-redundant selves available to the individual. The higher the number of non-redundant selves, the higher the individual's complexity and the more capable of cognitively buffering against stressors. This research is echoed (Simmons and Blyth, 1987; Mortimer and Call, 2001) with special emphasis on adolescence suggesting the more role-relationships and contexts the adolescent is engaged in, the better the adjustment and overall mental health. We posit the activity and goal of identity stasis through double-consciousness toward Black identity creates both a unique role relationship aspect and an inherent stress because of the socio-cultural elements that present themselves to Black people. This position is pronounced in considering self-complexity and identity for other groups and the significance is further highlighted when looking at consequent impact on general self and identity theory.

Winston (2004; 2007) asserts the self as complex, but stipulates that it is further complicated by race. In accord with this perspective, we contend that Black identity serves as a specialized aspect, a context dependent role relationship that is orchestrated with other identities within the self. And this negotiated fit contends with alignment to core mores and ideals of self. Harrell's (1999) Manichean psychology makes clear the challenge many Black Americans face in assuming authentic identities. This fit and subsequent balance is compounded for Black males because of unique pressures to assume and to reinforce representations that are misaligned with self because of conscious and unconscious pulls to fulfill social expectations (i.e. cool pose). Though there is not an optimal fit of Black identity for Black males in terms of society at large, there is an optimal fit for him based on the constitution of his personality and the context within which he is living—an authentic fit (Ryan et al., 2005).

Levin (1973) lends familiarity to this identity negotiation funneling the adoption of cultural norms through willing conformity where there is an organic fit between human needs and social norms; coerced conformity where personality and normative pressures produce incompatible behavioral demands; and normative pluralism where diverse norms exist that allow for norm and value match with personality.

The sophisticated blending of Black identity into other identities, self, culture and environment further illustrates the heavy work associated with identity stasis. The dynamic proves a type of identity coping mediated by identity stasis and resting at identity when a relative self-comfort that is dependant on situation and context is achieved. Notable is that Spencer et al. (2003) found identity as coping is demonstrative of a psychologically healthy sense of self and a healthy sense of self relative to others among Black adolescent boys when they employ culturally textured religion, spirituality and pride.

Coping is understood as a response aimed at diminishing the physical, emotional and psychological burden linked with stressful life events and daily hassles (Snyder and Dinoff, 1999). For present purposes, coping strategies are those that minimize psychological strain. As it relates to advancing identity stasis, coping is looked at in terms of styles (Harrell, 1979; Harding, 1975), motivation (Jones, 1997; 2003) and in the activity of simply being a Black male (Spencer, 1997; Stevenson, 2003). In referencing principles of a New Big Five in personality, coping can also be considered in terms of characteristic adaptation—perhaps the form of identity stasis—through culture. Each of these coping types requires psychic energy that has the ability to compromise or to enhance the self (Beaumeister, 1999). The extent to which this activity takes place depends on the individual's ability to facilitate an identity stasis that does not cause cognitive vacillation, limiting the amount of energy available to other identities within the self. This "doing" of identity (Cuningham, 1999; Spencer, Cunningham and Swanson, 1995; Stevenson, 2003), or identity striving, especially among Black males, is advanced with a different look at personality and its relationship to identity stasis.

Identity Stasis, Id, Ego and Superego

As McAdams and Pals (2006) provide the hard edges in terms of how the present analysis approaches personality, a glancing assumption of Freud's structural theory gives a starting point for the more malleable personality center of this theory and method development.

The id, ego and the superego are used to frame Freud's (1949) personality orientation. Operating from a pleasure, reality and moral principle respectively, shades of this approach are seen in the identity stasis to Black identity discussed previously allowing for a pragmatic connection to psychodynamic personality. Together with topography, the id, ego and superego provide organizational elements for identity stasis while side stepping the full implications of psychoanalytic theory.

Plainly, the id is that aspect of personality that derives energy from the physiological. It is an undifferentiated, instinctual level adjustment that is only concerned with personal survival and is manifest on the physical plane. The id functions to get the body fed, cleaned and appropriately stimulated. However, the id becomes less efficient as the organism's world expands. As such, it becomes necessary to employ a part of the personality that is effective in getting needs met in a world that is larger than a unitary world-view. Thus, an ego develops and facilitates getting needs met in a real world that includes other people and multiple resources. The superego offers a smoothing of the maturing personality and allows the person to function not only in a physical reality, but also in a social reality where there is a dictated moral dimension. This plane of right and wrong is navigated as safe spaces are found among other people that are, likewise, seeking to have their respective, complex needs met.

Identity stasis is most readily available to analysis as the ego emerges. Because of the requisite balance that must be struck between the instinctual needs of the id and the moral aspirations of the superego, context becomes relevant. We contend that this is especially the case for Black males because of both obvious and subtle demands to operate within a physical and moral reality that is complicated by race (Winston et al., 2004).

With these complex pulls on the self, identities look to safeguard the container from anxiety by coping through defense mechanisms. Here there is the possibility of unconscious activity. It may be necessary to conserve energy by immersing overly demanding emotional work into identity aspects that house behaviors that identity stasis must integrate. These aspects are thought to have incorporated into them some variation of the five primary defense mechanisms: repression, reaction formation, projection, regression, or fixation. This strategy of reducing anxiety would not presuppose the coping of styles (Harrell, 1979; Harding, 1975), motivation (Jones, 1997; 2003) and the activity of simply being a Black male (Spencer, 1997; Stevenson, 2003). It would be supplementary, attaching itself to one of these styles through topography—the conscious, preconscious and unconscious. For example, one of the participants in our analysis states:

> Coltrane.session.4: I feel like °you know° for me, like, I don't have a choice not to succeed . . . I have to do it . . . I mean I think I'm pretty smart, so, for some reason I feel like I gotta be right, like, when most of the time when I'm talking about stuff . . . I feel like (2.0) in succeeding I can't, you know, be wrong with it, being wrong would be kind of, like, bad.

The above narrative piece presented through the Jeffersonian Transcription System (appendix 2) frames Coltrane's simple and perhaps by some accounts unremarkable explaining of an identity of success. A consistent theme in his life story, this identity as coping is positioned in a racialized context (as is substantiated in chapter 4) balancing a societal expectation of him as Black male against a well-defined self-concept that refutes many common stereotypes. The felt need to "be right" because of his additional identification of self as "pretty smart" and the "gotta be right . . . I can't be wrong with it" positioning toward success suggests a coping that is very much in the conscious and preconscious and is planted within the realms of coping as motivation (Jones, 1997; 2003) and the activity of being a Black male (Spencer, 1997; Stevenson, 2003). But to paraphrase Freud, this articulation is the tip of the iceberg.

The preconscious and unconscious are of consequence as evidenced by what is not fully articulated. "In succeeding I can't, you know, be wrong with it, being wrong would be kind of, like, bad" illustrates that Coltrane has given himself very little margin for error because of his being a Black male, this congruent with demands from society that suggest to be wrong and to be Black demonstrate not capable and, ultimately, failure as reinterpreted by Coltrane. Though consciously recognizing a stereotypical representation of self that could even be internalized on some level, Coltrane engages in sublimation, an unconscious/preconscious drive toward the positive. Gordon (2004) might suggest prototypical defiance, achievement resulting from pressing through hardship and social stigma. Coltrane is driven to succeed through stereotype by being better than expected and by pushing to be better than all others. With this there is the assumption of identity stasis through burden of proof assumption.

Of course, Coltrane's brief narrative could also lend energy to the concept of stereotype threat, but this orientation is not embraced here and does little more than to give a reference point when looking at affirmative development.

Though not a central component of the present analysis, it is thought that the preconscious and unconscious motivation from anxiety related to failure is redirected into coping that would be evident in the other identities that are embraced, in what ways they are embraced and may have more well-defined exemplars of defense mechanisms.

The conscious is understood as the effortful awareness of situations and circumstances, while the unconscious represents automatic responses to stimuli (Bargh, 1997; Devine, 1989; James, 1890; Kihlstrom, 2001). With identity stasis synthesizing information such that a cohesive Black identity is achieved, the unconscious is of particular interest because of those things that contribute to the process of a racialized identity stasis without explicit awareness. The psychological unconscious (Kihlstrom, 2001) informs this specific identity stasis and affords it the incorporation of information such that there is the realization of what needs to be compromised or uncompromised based on semantic processing that can occur in the absence of conscious awareness (Kihlstrom, 2001; Bynum, 1999; Kambon, 1992). As a result of this apparent and implicit consciousness availed to a racialized stasis, the Black identity that results informs multiple dimensions and expressions (Cross, 1991; Sellers, 1997; 1998), and is interwoven with those aspects that comprise the self concept. In appreciating the activities associated with identity stasis and the resulting Black identity, a more direct connection from stasis to identity in relation to the self is available; this suggested in Coltrane's above articulation and in participant discourse presented in chapter 4.

The bifurcated experiences of participants in this analysis are understood through discourse. This commentary is not a psychodynamic extraction. It is an exploration of identity formation through an expression of a version of a worldview (van den Berg et al., 2003) and is informed by perspectives and theory that speak to the complexity of identity construction in general and identity stasis specifically.

Again, with selectively grounding identity stasis in Freud's personality and coping the interesting issues of the psychosexual stages of development are sidestepped, as they are unnecessary and perhaps even misleading given our intent. Identity stasis does not attach itself to full Freud, however, appreciating the above constructs provide valuable insight into possible avenues toward balance. Beaumeister's ego depletion and ego replenishment has utilized Freud in a similar fashion.

Ego depletion exists in the realm of the self's executive function which encompasses volition—choosing, deciding initiating action, exerting control over self and world and altering the self (Baumeister, 1999). Ego depletion occurs when there is too large a tax placed on the limited amount of energy attached to issues of volition. It is considered that the amount of tax placed on a Black American male adolescent in his reconciling double-consciousness through identity stasis toward the construction of self could cause ego depletion. With this, however, there is also the need to consider Ego-replenishment, the coping component after depletion occurs (Baumeister, 2002). Ego-replenishment is the building-up of the "muscle" that was strained as a result of depleting. Replenishment could come about in any number of ways including the integration of different styles (Harrell, 1979) or the assumption of a particular motivational aspect (Jones, 2003). Whatever the case, there is a resistance to the ego depletion occurring again if an effective coping mechanism is incorporated. This analysis posits that ego depletion and ego-replenishment can be found in life story narratives. In carefully considering the fashion by which narratives are constructed (McAdams 1999; 2001) there is the ability to figure how double-consciousness, the activity/goal of identity stasis and its impact on Black identity hang together and influence other self aspects. There is also an opportunity to use this active self-construction to illustrate how these young men use coping mechanisms to incorporate and to avoid stressful events highlighting ego depletion and ego-replenishment activity. With the life story serving as a psychological process of personality development within the field of narrative theory (McAdams, 1999), inroads in this phenomena coupled with the emphasis of context to the individual's interpretation of self and identity could aid in a more complete scope available for personality psychologists to draw conclusions in the analysis of trait and motivation based behavior.

In further linking personality and identity, the self proves a crucial link. Understanding personality as:

The dynamic organization within the individual of those psychophysical systems that determine his [sic] unique adjustments to his [sic] environment (Allport, 1954),

the self is pivotal in that adjustment. It is the real-world link to personality, promoting differential sampling, processing and evaluation of information from the environment and thus leads to differences in social behavior (Triandis, 1989). Accordingly, as a product of Black personality the Black American self assumes the role of mediator, constantly probing to adjust for racialized contexts, a default stitching in the fabric of the environment that Black Americans must negotiate. Considering the self in this context lends to a perspective that allows for the appreciation of the full complexity of the construct absent extremes and inclusive of fundamental psychological tenants frequently ignored in the understanding of Black identity.

As previously stated, identity is the structure representative of individual parts of the self. The self-concept is the particular domain of the self that identities make whole (Baumeister, 1986; Linville, 1985; 1987). This multiplicity that is kept whole by the self is in line with Mead's (1934) symbolic interactionism. The identities are the roles of one's personality via the self, or the smallest puzzle pieces to a personality that, for Black Americans, are informed by the racialized context in which one lives. The personality shapes the self, the self shapes the identity, which in turn operates in the environment to whatever degree and reinforces and/or modifies the self to the extent that it is able considering the rooting nature of personality. Accordingly, identity is both the core of the individual and at the core of the communal culture (Erikson, 1968).

Consequently, in an effort to further define identity stasis, it can be understood within a domino of psychological interconnectedness. Personality for the Black American is a personality that has attached a dynamic relation to the environment of racism. The self is defined such that the importance and relevance of what it means to identify as Black is understood within a racialized environment that implies poles because of a historical neglect given to the specialized question of Black identity. And identity stasis is the process by which an individual orchestrates identity balance racialized, and other, allowing for Black identity assumption, a Black personality and reconciling the afore mentioned poles of "American and Negro."

Identity Stasis and Black Personality

Identity Stasis, again, is the tool by which Black identity is achieved through the balance of bifurcated identities. Black identity, in turn, exists within the self concept as a permeating fundamental that impacts the functioning of other identities, or self aspects (Linville, 1985; 87) that contribute to the self system. Black identity is aptly positioned as scaffolding within the framework of one's central social constructs—race for example—in such a way that is either clearly accessible or invisible—conscious or unconscious—to the individual (Oyserman and Markus, 1996), depending on the fashion by which one assumes this identity. The self is the container within which identities are given the energy to manifest and the reconciling of double-consciousness through a racialized identity stasis provides the glue, the Black identity, that marshals other identities within the self concept toward the goal of identity stasis.

Also important in considering identity stasis is to do so in such a way that allows for the acknowledgement of the psychic hurdles associated with the context of racism, but not allowing this acknowledgement to equal the entirety of the Black American self. To this end Jones (1991) provides vigorous reasoning toward expanding the influences that impact Black personality, directly informing the conceptualization of Black identity and identity stasis.

The balance between how much one is drawn to express a personality consistent with an African/Black American cultural experience versus more squarely American mechanisms and characteristics is core to Black identity research and the understanding of identity stasis.

Understanding personality as a collective of enduring traits that allow individuals to effectively negotiate their physical, psychic and intrapsychic environment (Allport, 1954; Jones, 1991; Larsen and Buss, 2002; Kambon, 1992) is key to figuring the self and identity. Jones (1991) in his assertion of perspective on Black personality places the environment that Black Americans must negotiate as one replete with an ever-enduring racism. Black personality, then, is found in the ways in which one is able to assume and implement their traits and cognitive networks in dealing with racism. This analysis agrees with these politics of personality, acknowledging the legacy of slavery and racism as significant variables that must be dealt with in developing personality and associated self constructs. Particularly impacting in the Jones perspective (1991) is the analysis of how researchers factor racism in personality development among Black people.

Research in Black personality, often paralleling and at times overlapping Black self and identity research, focuses on thought that often mirrors tenants of deficiency models. In these instances there is more elaboration and focus on the potential for Black personality, however there is also a self-hate paradigm (Kardiner and Ovesey, 1951) versus more contemporary thought that emphasizes a secure Black identity that is almost exclusively group-oriented. This group identity is a reaction to the classic self-hate paradigm, indicating that though approached differently, the deficiency model persists as the foundation for both perspectives whereby the analysis of Black personality is steeped in pathological properties resultant from the racism Black Americans are charged to endure (Horowitz, 1939; Kardiner and Ovesey, 1951). Accordingly, rather than positing the personality of Black Americans from a culturally relativistic context, i.e. Manichean (Harrell, 1999) or in a field of racism (Jones, 2003;

2004), the norm is to place emphasis on the individual absent the intricacies of the psychological impact of racism. The norm is to view the individual as racism's victim or champion. This approach neglects the wide expanse of personality.

TRIOS theory (Jones, 2003) helps in providing a perspective that aids in the reconsideration of the extremes of Black American personality and affiliated identity. With cultural aspects that lean on Kroeber and Kluckhohn (1952), TRIOS is defined as a theory of culture and psyche. In utilizing the tenants of time, rhythm, improvisation, orality and spirituality, the theory, which assumes several aspects of the Triple Quandary's Afro-Cultural dimension (Boykin, 1986), allows for a multidimensional approach in how equilibrium might be achieved by Black Americans in a racialized society.

The polarities of expression that differ in the subjective or perceived value of the TRIOS dimensions determine the theory's intimate relationship to cultural racism (Jones, 1997). Given the realities and products of cultural racism visited on the targets of the phenomena, the cognitive responses beyond the traditionally simplistic self-hate and elaborated upon self-hate are allowed a more textured analysis through TRIOS. With TRIOS one can more comprehensively examine the formation of beliefs about the efficacy and competence of human beings as a function of their race, the influence of race on standards of beauty and body image and in personal and collective assessment of history and culture (Harrell, 1999)—again, the three distinct domains of cognitive activity that racism affects.

Field Theory frames TRIOS indicating the importance of context in its application. Influenced heavily by Lewin (1946), TRIOS positions context beyond the immediate environment by including the dynamic energy that helps navigate a person through that environment with direction, purpose and intention (Jones, 2003). In considering racism as the field in which Black Americans operate, complete with the cognitive dedication required, TRIOS provides domains that address personality formation more fully by attending to cultural foundations absent from traditional personality, self and identity theories.

A Complex Self and Race Self Complexity

Race self complexity (Winston et al., 2004; Winston, Philip, and Lloyd, 2007; Terry and Winston, 2007) extends from the TRIOS theoretical frame, proposing that race contributes to the complexity of the self system with a lens above or below the system and as a component within self layers. Identity stasis is related in that it is the process by which the component within the lenses of consequence develops and contributes to the self system through identity that is balanced with others.

Challenges that have historically presented with respect to the issue of identity are related to its relationship to the self. The question of the self, in turn, begins with determining its structure, content and function (Robins, Norem and Cheek, 1999) and whether the construct is a unitary or multifaceted entity. Most current studies accept the conceptualization of the self as having more than a single influence, or as being multidimensional (Sellers, 1998; Linville, 1987; Markus, 1977; Stryker, 1987). The present analysis adheres to this assumption.

Other issues of the self deal with definitions of self-knowledge, human potential and fulfillment, relation between the individual and society and self-definition (Baumeister, 1999; Cross, 1991; Stevenson, 2002). Emphasis here is on how race interacts with these issues as related to questions of identity, culture, achievement and the self-concept through the process identity stasis.

The three fundamental representations of the self-concept, the individual, relational and collective selves (Sedikides and Brewer, 2001; Brewer and Gaertner, 1996), help to provide additional substantiation of the complexity inherent in self and identity and offer other areas that the analysis of identity stasis must negotiate. In considering these representations, the bifurcated identities that Black Americans must negotiate are further charged to contend with unique traits, didactic relationships and group membership.

The self is fundamentally complex. That complexity is further compounded by race. This is the core of race self complexity. Understanding that recent findings related to human genome research suggests that there is no biological basis for race (Keita and Kittles, 1997), race self complexity contends phenotypic visibility and variation provide links between biology and the psychological functioning of Black Americans. Consequently, race self complexity posits a cultural historical and a biopsychological perspective by which race must be considered and that complexity adds further complexity to the self system both between the layers of the self and within the self system (Winston et al., 2004; Winston, Philip, and Lloyd, 2007; Terry and Winston, 2007).

There are five tenants of race self complexity. Primary among them are that within the United States there are macro and micro level environments that require that Blacks process information related to race and the personality of Black Americans can not be comprehensively understood without consideration of how individuals adapt to an environment of racism. Race self complexity also accepts the position that race has meaning in Black Americans' construction of their individual past, present and collective future selves (Jones 2003; Erikson, 1966). The meaning of race also has associated a requisite racism that is a psychological reality at any given time for Black Americans and informs a thematic psychological unity in self construction (Jones, 2003). In addition, race self complexity indicates that ego depletion/replenishment can be a consequence in the processing of race related information implicating general adaptations of Black Americans to the environment.

There are two primary perspectives of race self complexity. The biopsychological perspective suggests that because of phenotypic variation there is an associated psychological dealing that is traversed because of attitudes associated with melanin variation. The cultural historical perspective of race posits human development as a cultural process. Accordingly, unique historical experiences of Black people of African ancestry in the United States gives race psychological meaning that is incorporated into cultured patterns of thought, feelings and actions. Here both the biopsychological and cultural historical representations of race self complexity are considered in identity construction.

The Black Male and Adolescence

Bluntly, there are misfit answers to the question of the Black male adolescent. And because of this there is not an opportunity to fully consider his predicament and his propensity for affirmative development. For example, if we ask, simply, who is the Black adolescent male in America, typical responses are: he is separated from the whole of society, there are more Black males in the prison industrial complex than in college or there is a requisite hyper masculinity and bravado that factor into his identity. Initially these stereotypes seem to fit (as many stereotypes tend to without full consideration), but with the application of logical thought, there are spaces—the picture is incomplete. The responses are tantamount to giving three as the next term in a truncated Fibonacci sequence of one, two, not acknowledging the recursive pattern that is the basis for the sequence. One, one, two, three, five, eight . . . there is more—a systematized, meaningful more.

The fundamentals of this analysis lie within the realm of method and theory development because of gaps in research that can be addressed with respect to identity construction and a healthy focus on Black American adolescent males.

Most research conducted with Black adolescents within the United States positions them in some form of pathology or deficit (Gordon et al., 1995; Rice, 2004). In looking at non-pathological, "normal" Black adolescents, there is an opportunity to step toward a more comprehensive view of psychological functioning and to discover practical avenues that lead to healthy day-to-day living.

Research concerning Black adolescents also tends to view race as a categorical variable except when dealing with issues of identity development (Winston et al., 2004). As a result, the depth and consequence of being a young Black male in the United States is frequently neglected. With emphasis on context there is an ability to extend this narrow understanding in considering the nature of such a life.

Again, there is the assumption that the identity of Black Americans and of adolescents is particularly complex. Additionally, the environment in which young Black males must negotiate and develop identity is particularly sophisticated requiring method and theory that are capable of addressing much of that sophistication. In attending to method and theory development the current analysis is intended as contribution in addressing the complexities of the adolescent Black male's lived experience and identification. It is posited that a stretch beyond traditional or typical methods of research design, method and strategy are necessary because extant literature concerning Black adolescent males place them beyond the scope of normalcy. Accordingly, engaging in discourse analysis, critical discourse analysis, allows for an approach to understanding Black adolescent males that is inclusive of their experience, context, individuality and strengths. And this is done toward a greater end of looking at method and theory related to identity via identity stasis.

During adolescence the primary task is to develop identity (Erikson, 1968). It is a pivotal stage in the scheme of personhood and represents an important place from which to examine the interconnectedness of double-consciousness, identity stasis, Black identity, self complexity, ego depletion and ego-replenishment and It is a time where individuals begin to actively and complexly define who they are in accord with the human desire to maintain coherence and meaning (Erikson, 1966; McAdams, 1999). It is also a period prime for the examination of Black identity because of the socially contextualized environment in which the individual is naturally placed, school, where there is the necessity to figure fit with respect to the assumption of identities, among them the identity of racial affiliation. Given the requisite striving to achieve the identity's duty of providing structure, meaning, a sense of personal control, consistency and a gauge for personal potential, adolescence avails itself to the type of introspection, self-analysis and self-reporting that is elicited through the engaged case study approach used here.

Though it is the contention of many that identity is tantamount to "figuring" during adolescence, a time where there is the "working through" of identity versus identity confusion, (Erikson, 1966; 1968), there is also the understanding that adolescence is culturally dictated, rendering the assumption of identity dependant on the circumstance and context within which the individual is operating (Kroger, 1996; Erikson, 1966). Also, this analysis operates from the perspective that identity is continually formed, re-formed, figured and worked through and that this activity begins with adolescence.

Black American adolescents, largely because of the universal context of racism (Jones, 2003), are at a point in time where they are able to both realize and express identity. This contention is further supported when considering identity as a marriage of the developmental stage in the life of the individual with a historical period in time; a complementary of one's life history and history (Erikson, 1966). This research proposes that the Black American adolescent's life history is at a matured point in time where she or he would recognize a Black identity formation in terms of a sense of inner identity (Erikson, 1968).

Approaching the identity of the Black American adolescent from the perspective of child-in-activity-in-culture context would also bolster the thinking that there is an identity to be found in adolescence (Vygotsky, 1978; Miller, 2002). By the time one achieves the ages of fourteen through eighteen there is a construction of cognitive skills, most importantly a system of meaning and its psychological tools—a culturally constructed system of knowledge (Miller, 2002; Vygotsky. 1978) that would, again, suggest the formation of a Black identity within the Black American adolescent. This identity could prove particularly well defined for the Black American adolescent male because of the intensity with which context often intersects his lived experiences.

Black American adolescent males are at greater risk for experiencing ego-depletion/replenishment because of the exaggerated strains placed on them because they are young, male and Black American. Environmental risk factors, specifically more acute racialized contexts, serve as the major reasons for this heightened opportunity for ego depletion/replenishment to occur. This, as a result, makes the Black American adolescent male an important sample by which to consider the process of identity stasis, interrelated identities, self-complexity and ego depletion/replenishment. An effective strategy by which identity stasis can be considered is `through the examination of narratives.

Narrative Theory and Discourse Analysis

Narrative theories of personality explain that as individuals approach late adolescence, they create internalized narratives of self. The narrative serves as a means of internal sight, an autobiographical self that is able to make sense of external stimuli in terms of evaluation, categorization and subsidization and has the capacity to offer a continuity with past experiences, commentary on current concerns and a template for future actions (Singer, 1995). From the standpoint of new narrative theory in personality, the life story itself is at once a construct—a psychological phenomena that serves as a component of personality and psychological process that speaks directly to personality psychology (McAdams, 1999; 2001); it is also appreciated as a construction of identity. Conclusions made from the analysis of narratives via life stories advance the Stasis/Static Model of Identity Negotiation (figures 3.2–3.10) by highlighting the balance of bifurcated identities as represented in discourse.

With narrative theory as a backdrop, identity is something constructed to fulfill a psychological function, specifically to allow for psychological unity. It is an act carried out by an individual within a particular social context. For Black adolescent males it is a universal racialized context. Accordingly, identity construction is a psychological aspect of identity that allows for the better understanding of identity form and raises questions about function (Winston et al., 2004).

In connecting concepts, identity construction is an approach to understanding identity complexity that has a theoretical anchor that integrates narrative theories of personality, the internal life story and discourse analysis.

Discourse analysis focuses on the close analysis of talk and text. It concerns not only method, but is a perspective on the nature of language and its relationship to the central issues of social science (Wood and Kroger, 2000). Discourse analysis is a related collection of approaches to discourse that incorporate data collection and analysis and a set of metatheoretical and theoretical assumptions and a body of research claims and studies (Wetherell and Potter, 1992; Potter, 2003; van den Berg et al., 2003). Subsumed within discourse, text and talk, is language.

Language is a form of symbolism—of all forms it is the most highly developed, most subtle and the most complicated (Hayakawa and Hayakawa, 1990). Focus on language, therefore, is complex because of the nuanced nature of this very particular symbolism. Nonetheless, it is important to note that in psychology language is basis for the majority of research methods employed and types of data collected. Therefore, attending to language here is at once common and novel.

Language, text and talk are the pivotal pieces of discourse analysis and focus on it allows for identity to be understood as a tool versus an achievement. Noting the importance of both is important. Understanding identity as a tool makes the centerpiece of the analysis the action and interpretation of the action rather than focusing solely on the representation of identity in terms of what it "is" (Winston et al., 2004).

As such, it is critical that the purpose of identity stasis is interpreted on both surface and depth levels. Interpretive repertoires, a form of discursive analysis, help toward this aim. A concept that emerged within the study of the sociology of scientific knowledge, interpretive repertoires (Gilbert and Mulkay, 1984) came to be used first within social psychology. It refers to "a lexicon or register of terms and metaphors drawn upon to characterize and evaluate actions and events" (Potter and Wetherell, 1987, p. 138). Interpretive repertoires have also been described as "part and parcel of any community's common sense, providing a basis for shared understanding" (Edley, 2001, p. 198). They are used here to get closer to Black American adolescent males and to discover what they draw upon in constructing their identity and an understanding of who they are within context.

Interpretive repertoires are identified through careful reading and rereading of the discourse. The goal is to recognize the discursive resources that are used within people's talk, particularly images, metaphors or figures of speech. This requires the analyst to look beyond the obvious and common content of what is being said to the form and meaning of constructing a particular discourse. There is great attention paid to what is implied by the words and the context in which they are said. The interpretive repertoire is the naming that represents the meaning.

A contextualized rationale of justification has to be developed that both describes and explains the interpretive repertoire. This requires a combination of paraphrasing the context and content of what is said, as well as selecting the most relevant data points from the dialogue that illustrates the interpretive repertoire. This is the base upon which the discursive component of this analysis is based.

THREE

Model Development: Placing Constructs

The stasis/static model of identity negotiation is forwarded to bring clarity to the fundamental drive toward psychological balance as expressed in the process/state of identity stasis. The basis of the model is in a personality psychology that is integrative in nature and that has as core an attending to the whole person. The theoretical underpinnings of the stasis static/model mirror those of identity stasis theory, relying heavily on McAdams and Pals (2006) New Big Five, Du Bois's double-consciousness, Freud topography and context (Jones 1991; Lewin; McAdams and Pals 2006). The particulars, or representative constructs in the model, are within the universe of underpinnings, but are further contextualized by specifics relative to the Black male sample.

Accordingly, the self as comprised by self aspects (identities) and informed by context are given finer points by coordinating TRIOS theory, Cross's Nigrescence Model, the Triple Quandary, The Multidimensional Model of Racial Identity and Phenomenological Variant of Ecological Systems Theory (PVEST). These constructs lend perspective to the type of identity stasis active for the Black American adolescent males of concern and help in understanding the particular type of ego depletion and replenishment that might present. The stasis/static model reinforces identity stasis theory and the personality pursuit of how the individual person is like all other persons—this done by assuming a model applicable to all; how the individual person is like some other persons—as explored through racialized constructs that are applicable to many; and how the individual person is like no other person, which is to be explored through potential, intrinsic case study (Kluckhohn and Murray, 1953; McAdams and Pals, 2006).

As is implicit in a universal context of racism (Jones, 2004; 2005), phenotypic variation yields biopsychological and cultural historical factors that play heavy into how individuals identify and are identified racially (Winston et al., 2004; Winston, Philip, and Lloyd, 2007; Terry and Winston, 2007). Consequently, the ways that individuals find psychological balance given race will vary, but will present. A path toward the stasis/static model is found, for our sample, in the degree to which racial identity finds relevance with within the self and how that identification impacts other identities such that there is either co-operation and facilitative unity or aspect isolation and potential ego depletion. In order to help articulate the connections this analysis proposes between psychological constructs, the Stasis/Static Model of Identity Negotiation (as outlined in chapter 1) illustrates hypothesized interactions. The model suggests how identity stasis is coalesced with Race Self Complexity, self-complexity, identity (Linville, 1985; 1987, Rafaeli-Mor, 1999; 2002), Black identity (Cross, 1971; 1996; Vandiver, 2002, Sellers, 1997; 1998, Kambon, 1992) and ego depletion/replenishment (Baumeister, 1998; 1999; 2000).

Race Self Complexity serves as a conceptual beginning for identity stasis. The imperative of race as a real and consequential factor in how Black Americans define themselves, in the complexity associated with that racialized definition and in the further complication of the self pushed the idea of identity stasis forward. Though not race specific, identity stasis is defined through example by Race Self Complexity and is linked by it to a current and substantial model of Black identity, the Multidimensional Model of Racial Identity (MMRI).

In rooting the Stasis/Static Model, significant cues are taken from foundational studies in Black identity as Black identification is our sample's response to a universal context of racism. It is the most salient of identities that is to be negotiated into the self among this instrumental group of Black adolescent males.

The MMRI is a significant stride in Black identity theory that stresses a complex Black identity. Synthesizing the strengths of mainstream and underground research, exemplified most cogently in the writings of Gordon Allport (1954) and W. E. B. Du Bois (1903) respectively, the MMRI approaches Black identity from a multiple-influences perspective (Sellers et al., 1997; 1998). These influences are referred to as dimensions. A conceptualization derived from identity theory (Stryker and Serpe 1994) that explains an individual as having a number of identities that are hierarchically ordered. The MMRI shares this position emphasizing that race is but a single ordered identity to be fit, or balanced, with others within the self.

The multidimensionality of the Sellers model is of primary importance to Stasis/Static. It suggests an ability to explore issues of Black identity and associated self structures in greater depth and provides a logical connect to the self-complexity aspect of the model.

Nigrescence provides identity stasis a different look given a complexity couched within a stages. The foundational effort in psychology to advance Black identity toward new perspectives, Nigrescence is fundamental in a variety of Black identity studies (Marks et al., 2004; Parham and Helms, 1981; Milliones, 1976; Phinney, 1992; Parham, 1985; Sellers, 1997; Cokley, 2002; Vandiver, 2002; Kambon, 1992).

When first presented (Cross, 1971), the Negro-to-Black Conversion Experience posited that an optimal Black identity was achieved at the end of an individual's negotiating through a five-stage developmental model, each stage representing a different Black identity assumed. The stages were based on the individual's responses and behaviors around the phenomena of racism within the United States. The attention to racism present in the Cross model is consistent with our emphasis on recognizing the impact race has on the construct of identity for our sample. Aside from the fact that Nigrescence is the seminal work on Black identity in psychology, the model is important in present analysis and model development because it sets a mark for negotiating race, we contend, in a space that is largely personality dependent. In extrapolating Cross's Black identity to our model the phasic nature is suspended focusing on Nigrescence stages in terms of dimensionality.

Nigrescence stages are Pre-encounter, where race is incidental and there is more attending and focus on other group membership. Encounter is descriptive of the stage where there is an experience that has the individual re-consider their relation to Black culture and its positioning within society. Immersion-Emersion has the person embracing "Black" and refuting "White," though not psychologically committed to Black identification. Internalization positions the individual as Black and other, suggestive of a stasis state where there is psychological balance between Black and other group membership. And with Internalization-Commitment the person has embraced their Black identity, fitting it into the larger social order and incorporating humanity and broad commitments to personhood.

From the initial conceptualization of Nigrescence (Cross 1971, 1976) to its consistent reconsideration by Cross (1991, 1996;) and others (Vandiver et al., 2002), there is maturation and sophistication added with respect to the types of inquiry sought with its utilization (Cross, 2004). Nonetheless, theoretically, the revised Nigrescence maintains the pre-encounter, encounter, immersion-emersion, internalization-commitment stages, with refinement to the particulars of each.

Again, the negotiation of a Black identity is a fundamental characteristic of the Cross model that informs Stasis/Static. With the activity Nigrescence demands, there is both stasis and static that has the ability to cognitively tax to the point of ego depletion. How an individual deals with these demands, or the inability to—the expanding and contracting pupil of TEM (figure 3.1)—is often dependent on the interplay of person and environment. Spencer's Phenomenological Variant of Ecological Systems Theory (PVEST) gives a point of departure to better deal with the issue of dynamic blending and its role in identity negotiation for both the Sellers and Cross models. It proves vital in our model development in its extension of context and in allowing for measured reason behind the impact of environment on identification and balance versus imbalance.

The utility of PVEST lies in its ability to highlight the interaction that exists between the self and the cultural context. PVEST rests on the assumption that feedback from different cultural contexts will influence self-perceptions. These self-perceptions influence how an individual will adapt to similar cultural contexts across the life span. These self-perceptions will also influence which behaviors or attributes an individual chooses to emphasize or downplay. The self-perception of an individual also influences the reactive coping methods used in stressful situations. These coping methods have the possibility of becoming stable coping methods that an individual will use across the life span to deal with similar contexts. Though all reactive coping methods are intended to be successful and healthy, individuals who are engaged in high risk environments often develop maladaptive coping mechanisms that are not appropriate across different cultural contexts. This is where Identity Static might manifest.

With PVEST Spencer et al. (1997) asserts that not only does the processing of phenomena and events influence the value that one feels for himself, but also the way in which one gives meaning to different aspects of themselves. Specifically, one's perception of experiences in various cultural contexts will influence how he perceives himself. Spencer posits that these "perceptual processes" are dependent upon social cognitive skills. These self-perceptions also include reactive coping methods to stress. These problem-solving strategies are linked to specific stressors in a cultural context. The repetitiveness of the cultural stressors allows for the formation of stable coping responses, which take the form of emergent identity or self-processes, or identity stasis and ego-replenishment in cases where ego depletion might have been present.

The TRIOS theoretical orientation, as discussed in chapter 2, helps to frame the universal context of racism within which the Stasis/Static Model is based–it situates the broad environment that the Black male adolescent has to cope with as explained through PVEST. Additionally, the dimensionality of TRIOS as represented by time, rhythm, improvisation, orality and spirituality, contribute to the paradigm of self-complexity that this analysis contends and suggests a resiliency, or defiance, of the Black American psyche (Jones, 2004).

TRIOS is presented as the combined coping, communication and group processing of Black Americans that finds base in multiple African societies (Jones, 2004). It is given that there will be variation in the identification one has with TRIOS depending on how their personality adjusts relative to their particular racialized environment and their interpretation of it. This non-idealized Black identification is similar to MIBI as is the dimensionality and serves as a bridge, of sorts, to the basic aspects of self-complexity.

Self-complexity as defined by Linville (1985; 1987) explains the concept as the dimensionality underlying the self-concept or the degree to which individuals are able to differentiate knowledge about the self. Again, the self-concept is the component of the self that is defined as a cognitive schema; an organized knowledge structure that contains traits, values, episodic and semantic memories about the self and controls the processing of self-relevant information (Campbell et al., 1996). Quantity of self-aspects and overlap of theses aspects, or lack thereof, is key to the level of self-complexity assumed. The more complex individual is the one who is able to have a high number of non-redundant selves to refer to. The model finds its historical base in cognitive structure models of the 1950s and 1960s. Specifically in the work of Kelly's (1955) personal constructs and Bieri's (1966) work surrounding individual's perceptual system. Both suggest the importance of differentiation and integration also noted as cornerstone in Nigrescence, the Multidimensional Model of Racial Identity, TRIOS and PVEST.

In considering self-complexity, there is also distinction to made between multiple selves (identities) and identity enactments. Cross considers enactments as of a consistent singular identity that is manifest dependent on exacting activities. The enactments would, in essence, parallel the selves. What does this mean for identity stasis? It might suggest that adaptation to the enactments would be gauged by the individual such that Black identity would remain in a place such that ego depletion would not take toll on the cognitive abilities of the individual. Alternatively, if identity stasis is not achieved, consistent, differentiated adaptations would tax the individual compromising overall identity balance. It is also important to stipulate that ethnic identification is not always tied to discrimination. In the instances where one is able to be open and full, not self-conscious relative to race, there may be an opportunity to build a cognitive reservoir that is racially sensitive and able to solidify an ego–replenishment that is durable to racialized enactments that allow for a racialized identity stasis and a cognitive buffer against negative or stressful racialized enactments.

Ego depletion/replenishment (Baumeister et al., 1999) finds space in the current model through the level of commitment the individual attributes to Black identification and related coping within the universal context of racism that must be negotiated. As expressed by Baumeister (1998; 1999; 2000), ego depletion is a tax placed on the self in negotiating the reality of the external world by mediating between conflicting inner and outer pressures. For this analysis it is thought that the assumption of Black identity at a high level of commitment that Stryker and Serpe (1994) emphasize as paramount in hierarchical ordering, an ordering that is also inherent in self complexity (Linville, 1985; 1987), has the ability to tax the limited amount of energy that the self has in its assumption of the executive function and issues of volition, thus impacting self complexity and associated behaviors.

Ego depletion and its possible effect on self-complexity provide a special concern within the context of racism. As previously explored through the explanation of TRIOS and field theory in the development of a Black identity (Jones, 1991; 2003), negotiating racism is a situation that is ever-present making the assumption of a balanced and cohesive self challenging in an environment that does not foster cultural norms. With this the Triple Quandary (Boykin 1986; 1995) provides a unique utility in the further understanding of Black identity particularly as it relates to self-complexity.

As discussed in chapter 2, the Triple Quandary is a theoretical framework that posits Black Americans as having three realms of social experience that must be negotiated within the dominant culture of America (Boykin 1986; Boykin and Ellison 1995). These realms specify a pursuit of mainstream goals and ideals that are pushed forward by the dominant group, the identification with other oppressed people such as the indigenous American, those of Hispanic heritage and others and a connect with the very specific socio-cultural history of Black Americans. An individual's participation in each of these realms occurs to varying degrees. Ultimately, the sum of a person's participatory experiences in each of these three areas formulates one's identity as a Black American in society. The realms are mainstream experience, the minority experience and the Afro-cultural experience respectively and all are multifaceted, echoing both the multiplicity of the self as it relates to identity and self-complexity.

Adherence to the realms presented is in the form of orientation or involvement, indicating that there is either some active participation in a particular domain or there is an experience about it. As it relates to Linville's (1985; 1987) self-complexity, the Triple Quandary has a direct influence on the ability of an individual to attend and to balance associated realms, consequently impacting the commitment to a Black identity, affecting the multiple selves able to be assumed which speaks to the balance of Black identity with other important aspects of the self.

Both Black identity and self-complexity can be considered coping mechanisms; Black identity because of its development largely as a fashioned response to racialized oppression (Cross 1996; Nghe and Mahalik 2001) and self-complexity because of the ability to cognitively buffer against stress (Rafaeli-Mor, 2002; Linville 1985; 1987). But rather than suffice as the entire self-concept as is frequently suggested, Black identity is most sensibly positioned as mandatory fundamental, to whatever degree, within a larger self-concept. Self-complexity accounts for this Black identity, perhaps, in that it represents a special dimensionality of the self-concept. Thus, Black identity within this framework is a perspective by which traits, values, episodic and semantic memories are considered and a racialized identity stasis is the negotiation of bifurcated experiences toward Black identity and the internalization of norms such that the Black identity manifest is capable of achieving coherence and equilibrium through further identity stasis.

The following figures are graphic representations of the Third Eye Model of Identity Negotiation, the subsequent Stasis/Static Model of Identity Negotiation and an Identity Stasis coping sequence. These represent the conceptual core of the present text.

Third Eye Model of Identity Negotiation

Self-Complexity, the dimensionality of the self-concept. The pieces of the whole of the self-concept also referred to as self-aspects.

Self-Concept, cognitive schema that is a component of the self; an organized knowledge structure that contains traits, values, episodic and semantic memories about the self and controls the processing of self-relevant.

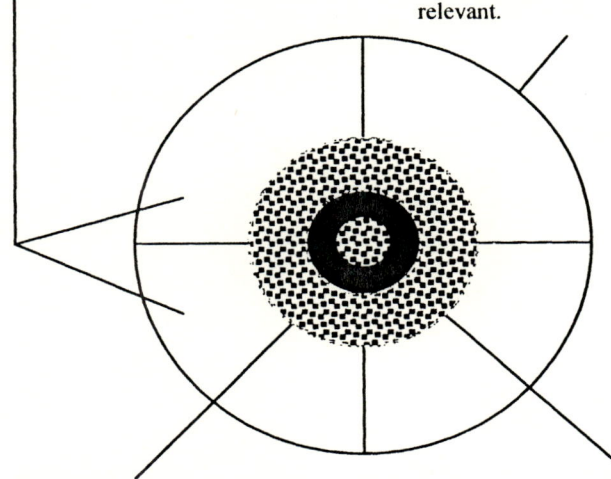

Ego depletion/Replenishment, psychic tax on the self resulting from the mediation of inner and outer pressures. Substantive focus is on the executive function. Extremes in Black identity trigger ego depletion or reinforce ego replenishment, which impacts self-aspects. As the Black identity pupil expands into the ego depletion membrane, ego depletion occurs. Ego depletion/replenishment in this model, then, is correlated to the process of a racialized identity stasis and the negotiation of environment/context.

Black Identity, product of the process of a racialized identity stasis. The extent to which the Black identity pupil is large/small is the extent to which self-aspects are impacted.

Figure 3.1. Initial thinking toward Identity Stasis

The Stasis/Static Model of Identity Negotiation

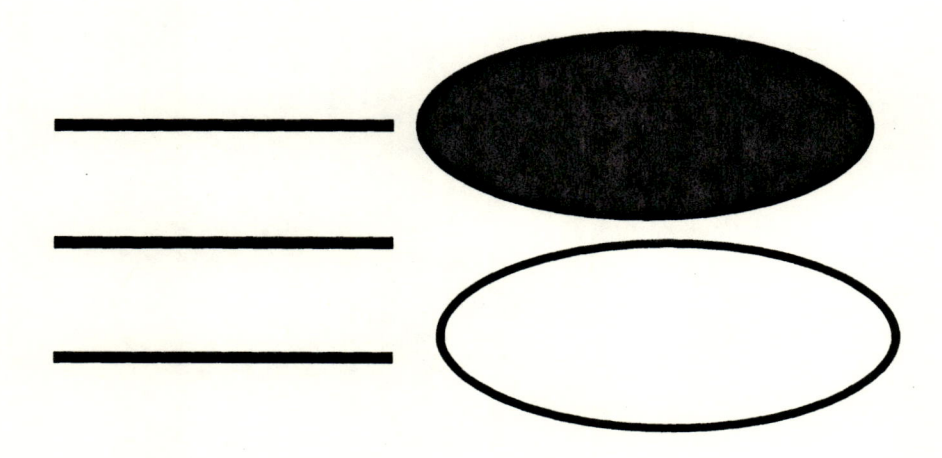

Figure 3.2. *Race Self Complexity* within lines of context. A theory of personality that attends to how race adds complexity to the individual and is particularly concerned with understanding the racialized self (Winston et al., 2004; Winston and Kittles, 2005; Maddox, 2004; Rice, 2004). Ovals represent a phenotypic ink (shaded oval) that is negotiated within the self-concept (open oval) that orchestrates the self-concept's non-redundant identities; this done within one self container.

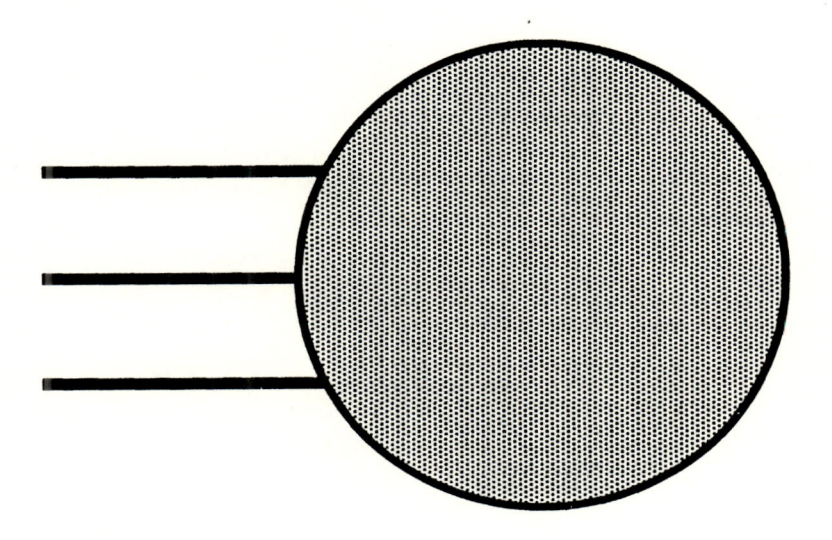

Figure 3.3. *Self Concept* with context suggested as of consequence. The circle whole is representative of an orchestrated race self complexity (figure 3.2)—the one self container—a cognitive schema, organized knowledge structure that contains traits, values, episodic and semantic memories about the self that controls the processing of self-relevant information.

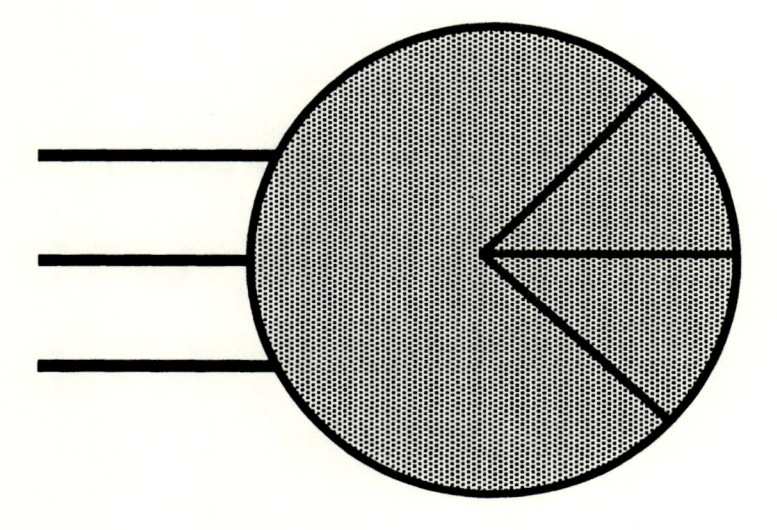

Figure 3.4. *Self-Complexity* with context suggested as of consequence. Segmented pieces of the circle represent dimensionality of the self-concept. These non-redundant identities are also referred to as self aspects. This complex nature of the self is further complicated with the introduction of phenotypic variation—race. Context informs the self and affiliated identities and the affiliated identities and the self, in turn, inform the context. The ability to balance this dynamic blending determines identity stasis/static. The extremes of stasis and static then determine the psychic tax on the individual or lack thereof—ego depletion or replenishment.

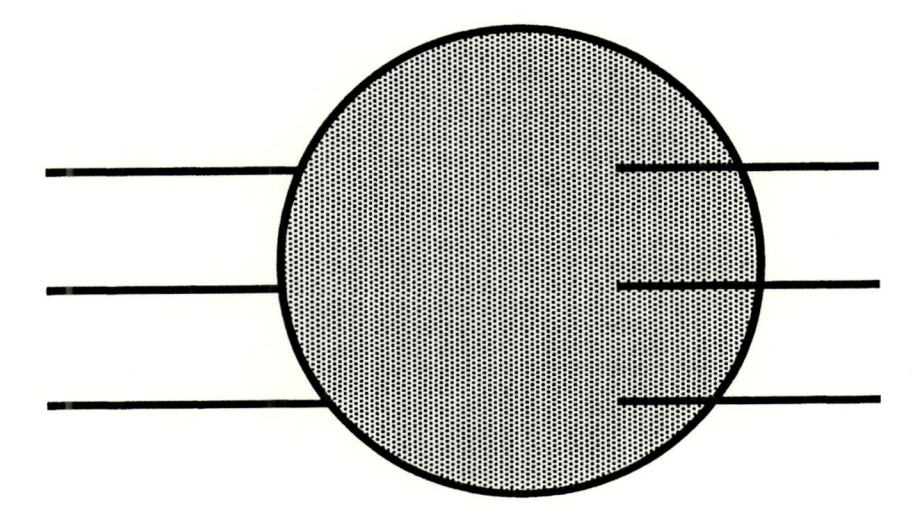

Figure 3.5. *Identity Stasis and Ego Stability/Replenishment* as suggested by self and context interplay. Straight horizontal lines between self and context demonstrate identity stasis—balance between the self-concept, related identities and the environment. Such balance suggests ego stability or replenishment. A psychic tax on the self, preventing it from mediating inner and outer pressures, is inconsequential because it does not exist or because effective coping has occurred in response to instances of ego depletion.

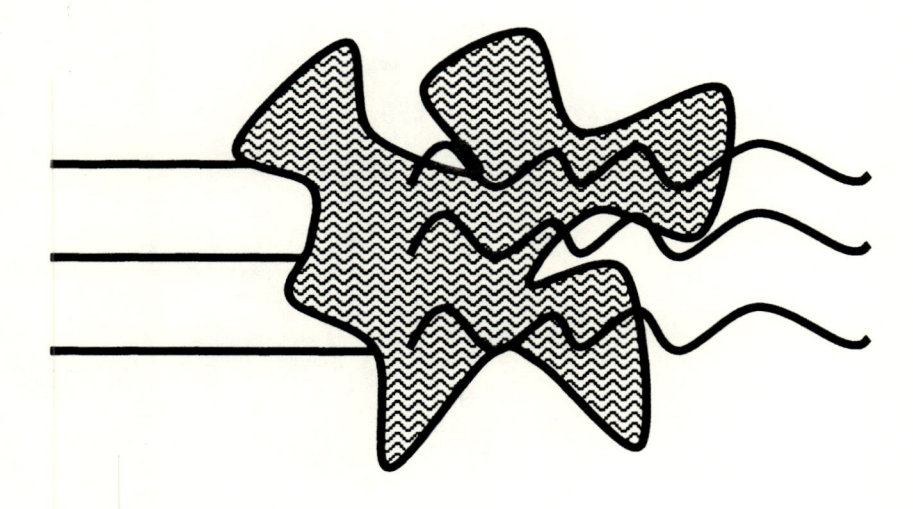

Figure 3.6. *Identity Static and Ego depletion* as suggested by self and context interplay. Waved horizontal lines between self and context indicate identity static—dissonance between self, related identities and the environment. Such dissonance suggests ego depletion, a psychic tax on the self—specifically the self's executive functioning—that prevents the self from most effectively mediating inner and outer pressures.

Identity Stasis

Environment/Context is balanced with self whole

The Self as comprised by identities/self-aspects

Identities/Self Aspects that comprise the self

Cognitive Energies that are dynamically blended to goodness of fit between identity and environment/context

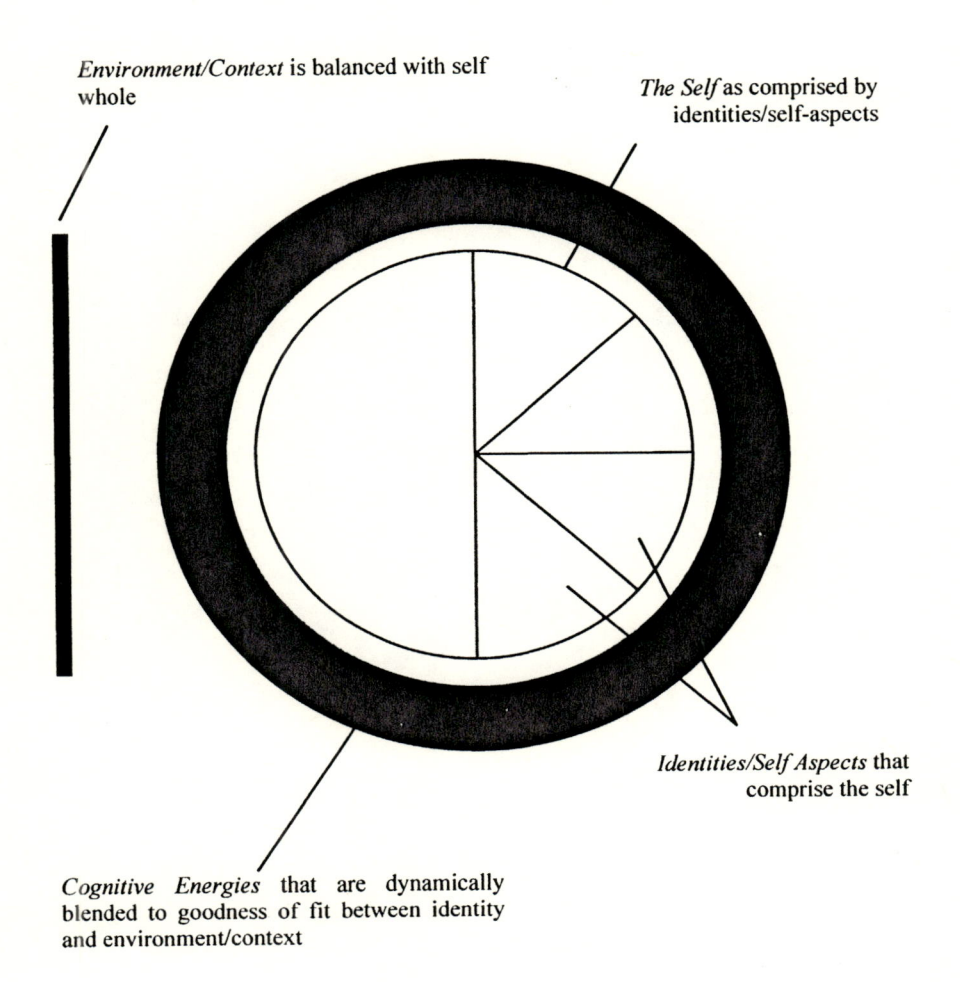

Figure 3.7. Identity balance as represented sans context, within a proverbial vacuum.

Identity Stasis Activity, Depletion

Environmental/Contextual Demands on self and associated identities

Identities/Self Aspects that comprise the self

Agentic Activity toward environmental/contextual demands in order to maintain and to stabilize identities and self

Potential for Depletion, opportunity for identity imbalance because of compromised cognitive energies available to the self

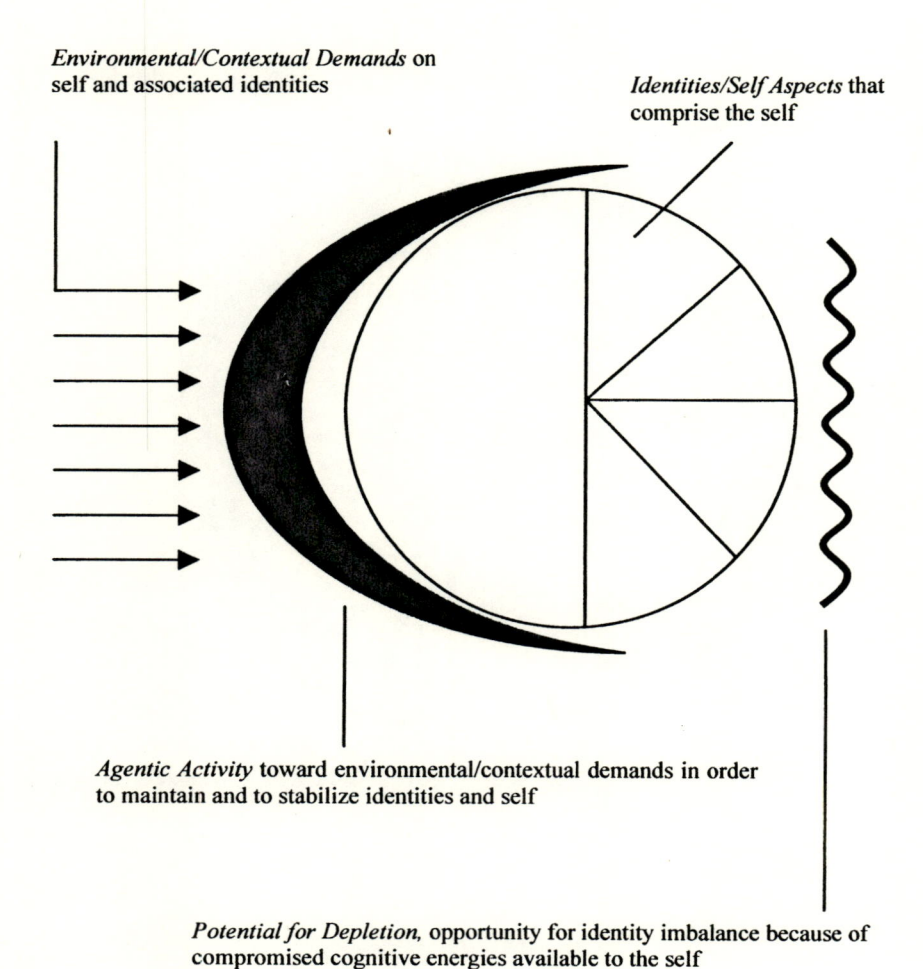

Figure 3.8. Activity of identity balance with potential for ego depletion.

Identity Stasis Activity, Replenishment

Environment/Context that is balanced, a negotiated goodness of fit with environment; identities are balanced within self

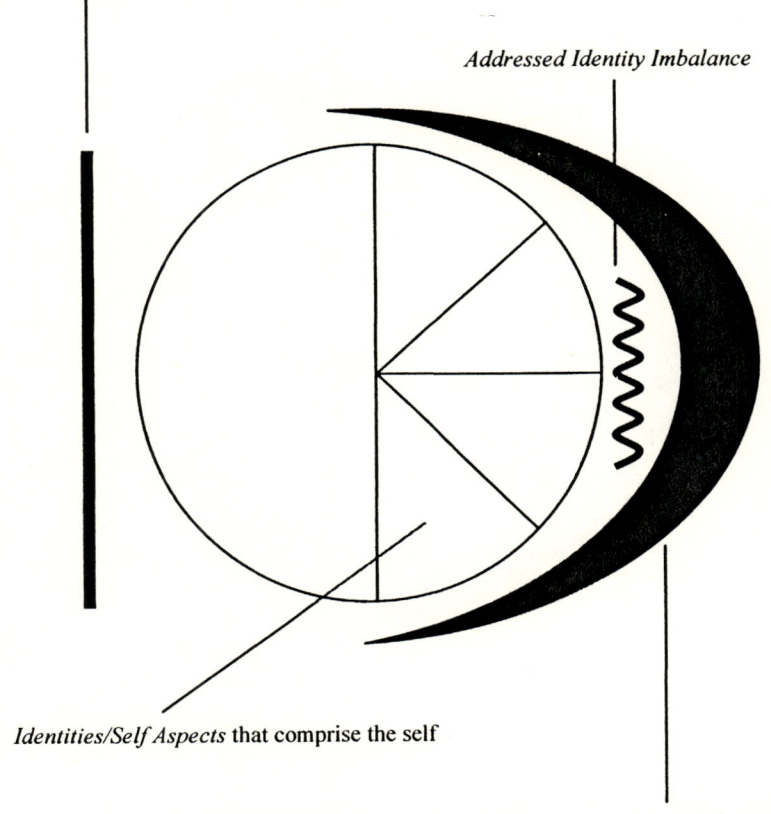

Addressed Identity Imbalance

Identities/Self Aspects that comprise the self

Shifting of Cognitive Energies from one environment/contextual demand to another; the re-suring of identities and self with developed coping/balance—ego replenishment

Figure 3.9. Activity of identity balance with potential for ego-replenishment.

Identity Stasis Activity

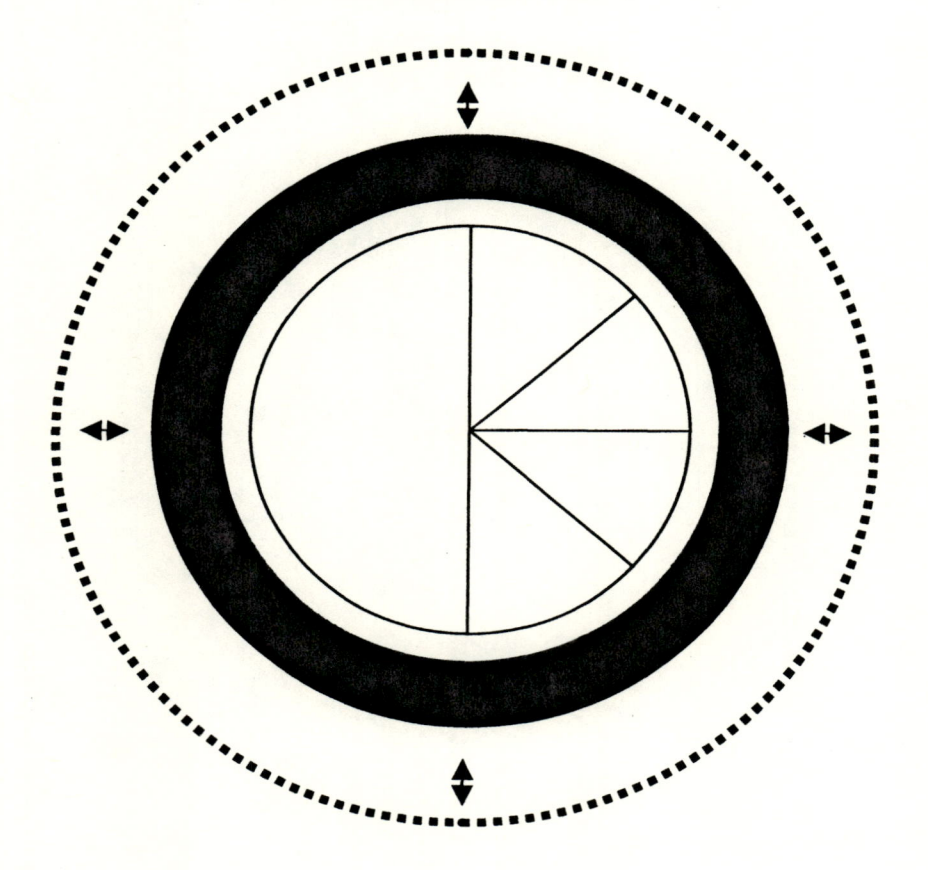

Figure 3.10. Identity balance as represented within context. Cognitive Energies are, again, dynamically blended to goodness of fit between identity/self and environment/context

FOUR

Orchestration

> You cannot open a newspaper without being offended. You cannot see a movie without being offended. What gets covered, how it gets covered, what's in *The Washington Post*, what vignettes in the Black community are described and what are left undescribed, how these decisions are made . . . It is a daily visitation of slights for African Americans. And it makes for us this preoccupation with race a necessary defense reflex . . . It's involuntary but necessary to survive.
>
> Robinson, 1998

The identity construction of the Black American males in this analysis was inherently complex. Performing critical discursive analysis on segments of data extracted from focus groups, identity stasis was interpreted as being represented in the complex construction of identity through narrative. There were three forms of identity stasis interpreted from selected segments of focus group data: (1) Identity Dilemma Articulation; (2) an Unadulterated Presentation of Self; and (3) Burden of Proof Assumption. As explained in Appendix One, this naming of the forms of identity stasis emerged from an iterative analytic process that included initial reading, data selection and characterization that helped the interpretation of identity stasis in the identity construction across focus group persons. The following is an extended defining of identity stasis through example and the activity of discourse analysis.

Identity Dilemma Articulation

Within discourse, Identity Dilemma Articulation is a form of identity stasis that is closely aligned with Du Bois's (1897; 1903) conceptualization of double-consciousness. As a form of identity stasis, Identity Dilemma Articulation is the realization of a bifurcation of identity that creates a dilemma. This bifurcation of identity is interpreted through the realization and explanation of the twoness that the individual is charged to negotiate within the universal context of racism (ISRL, 2004).

> Coltrane.session.6: I was talking about, like, Black identity and stuff. And like if you wanna, you can't really keep your identity and try to (0.2) like (0.5) to like be successful, it's not, it's not that easy because, you know like, America doesn't really accept (0.3) Black people, you know (0.5) like (1.0) in that, like

(1.0) since always that's, that's why like there's racism, you know? That's like because (0.5) Europeans thought we were inferior and that's why, you know, like their, they just thought their culture was just so, superior to ours and that's why we are always (1.0) like you know that's how like our culture isn't accepted here. That's why, you gotta go get a suit if you want a job and you can't be, °what else what was going to say? (heh, heh, 3.0)

Identity Dilemma Articulation is represented in the person's discourse throughout the entire data segment above. Evidence for this is provided by an evolving and stacked interpretation. Beginning the analysis with the locutionary or referential meaning, the person addresses Black identity and success[ful]. Apart from the task of discussing identity, the person seems to be positioning "Black identity" against trying to be "successful." One interpretation of the bifurcation of identity is that there is a twoness that is created by a dilemma related to "Black identity" and "success." The person indicates you "can't keep your identity and try to like to be successful." This analytic interpretation of the identity dilemma introduces the need to unify two identities, one that is at once "Black" and "your[s]" and one that is in line with success or perhaps more importantly "America[s] . . . accept[ability]."

An alternative interpretation of the bifurcation of identity is that the twoness is a result of a conflict between being able to "keep your Black identity" and "European thought" of Black people being "inferior." The nature of the dilemma is that success lies in the realm of "European thought" and such thought views Black culture and therefore Black identity as "inferior." Consequently, the pervading dilemma is most likely between maintaining one's Black identity in a universal context of racism in which "Europeans thought we were inferior . . . like their, they just thought their culture was just so, superior to ours." There is an emphasis in identity dilemma that seems distinct; there is "Europeans . . . culture" and "ours" setting a mark for the separation that the person describes between Black culture and the mainstream or White culture.

In reference to "Black identity," the person describes the entity as something "you can't really keep." This assertion is done first in relation to "be[ing] successful". The initial statement, however, is reframed as the person suggests that "Black identity" could possibly be maintained, indicating, "it's not that easy." The balance between "you can't really keep" and "it's not that easy" demonstrates that the person is negotiating "Black identity." The process is fluid as an example of the negotiation that is central to Identity Dilemma Articulation.

The passage could also be interpreted as a realization of identity stasis—a restatement for clarity where the person realizes that Black identity can be kept but not without effort. It cannot be kept in the sense of just being. There is activity, agency, a process that must be assumed as indicated by "and try to (0.2) like (0.5) to like," where there is a continuation of thought and "try" is an articulation of agency. It may be that the individual who is betwixt a mainstream and Black cultural identity realizes that they are active in engaging in the identity stasis process. This engagement may be something the individual may or may not have the ability to negotiate. Agency can further be interpreted by the linguistic patterns of pauses that suggest thought processing; pauses can indicate cognitive work (Wood and Kroger, 2000). This is especially likely when coupled with the filler utterances of four "like[s]" in the relatively restrictive space of twenty-seven words.

In beginning a pattern with respect to the explanation for a bifurcation of identity, the person adopts a position on why there is a negotiation of twoness in "keep[ing] your identity." Given that, "America, doesn't really accept Black people" there is a need for him to assume an identity other than one that is exclusively "Black," because that identity—that part of him—is not accepted in the "America" in which he lives. Again, Identity Dilemma Articulation serves as an appropriate interpretation of this process because of an outlining of the reasons for the negotiation(s) requisite for success.

The position adopted concerning why there is a negotiation of twoness in "keep[ing] your identity" is couched within a universal context of racism. This "America" that "doesn't accept Black people" has done so "since always . . . that's why, like, there's racism." This represents a position related to time that is fundamental in the experience of a universal context of racism. Jones (2003) argues that racism is a psychological reality at any given time and consists of the individual's personal as well as collective racial pasts and futures and their construal of the racial nature of their immediate experience.

The bifurcation of identity that represents Identity Dilemma Articulation is further extended to a physical manifestation of negotiation as the person assumes the position that "you gotta go get a suit if you want a job." The dilemma could be interpreted as the need to add on, dress up or to present differently, if there is the task of being accepted by the mainstream. The "suit" serves as a symbol for a white cultural norm; it is the costume or mask that is the container for all those white things that will allow for disguise and safe passage into European "accept[ability]." An alternate interpretation of this data is that the "suit" is reference to society and within this discourse could represent the adolescent expression of not wanting to conform to its standards.

Max extends the identity dilemma articulation in the co-construction of identity below:

Max.session.6: I mean. Uh. It's like (.shih, 0.2), we have to follow the White people's standard (0.3) you know? °and make our own standards below them. So we have to follow their standards and try to (2.0) like (3.5) follow after them (0.5) you know, the way to be successful because society looks up to the White people.

Yeah, um, as I was telling, it's like (0.5) society expects Blacks to follow African . . . I mean (4.0) okay (0.5) Blacks, I mean Blacks are supposed to like (1.5)

I think that White people are, like, the model of success and that's where we have to follow after, to like get opportunities in life

'Cause we always got to work twice as hard to prove them wrong, you know? (1.0) And also it's, like, hard to be yourself and who you are because sometimes (1.2) you have to change it up. Like (2.0) acting different (0.5) you know? (0.5) like (1.0) not say stuff you would normally say.

The bifurcation of Identity Dilemma Articulation is represented in the person's indication that "we have to follow the white people's standard and make our own standards." The dilemma lies in the fact that the two standards to be negotiated represent the Black cultural, or "our own standards" and the success oriented, or "the white people's standard." The positioning of the statements by the person suggests that the two "standards," or identities are mutually exclusive and hierarchical as denoted by the use of the word "below." Black standards and White standards represent the twoness the person has to negotiate within the universal context of racism inherent in Identity Dilemma Articulation.

Max.session.6: I mean. Uh. It's like (.shih, 0.2), we have to follow the White people's standard (0.3) you know? °and make our own standards below them. So we have to follow their standards and try to (2.0) like (3.5) follow after them (0.5) you know, the way to be successful because society looks up to the White people.

Yeah, um, as I was telling, it's like (0.5) society expects Blacks to follow African . . . I mean (4.0) okay (0.5) Blacks, I mean Blacks are supposed to like (1.5) I think that White people are, like, the model of success and that's where we have to follow after, to like get opportunities in life

'Cause we always got to work twice as hard to prove them wrong, you know? (1.0) And also it's, like, hard to be yourself and who you are because sometimes (1.2) you have to change it up. Like (2.0) acting different (0.5) you know? (0.5) like (1.0) not say stuff you would normally say.

The negotiated bifurcation of identity definitive of Identity Dilemma Articulation is further manifest in the person's discourse where "white people are . . . the model of success." Adopting the position that there is a "model" further reinforces the twoness of not simply having two standards, "our own" and "white people's standards," but also is suggestive of incongruence, a non-fit. This could be interpreted as evidence of Identity Dilemma Articulation and a process of identity stasis that requires the negotiation of two identities. There is a compatibility or fit with respect to the base, Black identity and an incompatibility or non-fit, relative to the "model of success" that represents identity bifurcation and the associated dilemma to be balanced. As a result of this mis-fit the person exercises some agency positioning himself as one who is to "follow." In terms of the locutionary or referential meaning, because "white people are the model of success" non-whites must, actively, "follow after" them to "get oppor-

success" non-whites must, actively, "follow after" them to "get opportunities in life."

When the speaker uses the linguistic declarative "I think" he indicates ownership of these beliefs. A surface interpretation of the discourse suggests that the person accepts this reality within a universal context of racism and has set a plan to negotiate the bifurcated identity presented.

However, in fully interpreting the meaning of "I think" it is important to look at the stutter start and shifts within the context of the entire data segment. These linguistic devices may serve to frame the utterances that follow and are, thus, important to interpret for relevance to the person's explicit identity dilemma declaration. What comes before "I think" is a variety of stammered and shifting thought data that describe what "society expects." Consequently, it appears that the person could be fully realizing his constructed thought, his Identity Dilemma, indicating a belief that society expects Blacks to "think that white people are the model of success." This could be interpreted to suggest, then, that it is not what the person thinks but what "society" thinks.

As has been the case with previously interpreted discourse, stammering associated with initiating ideas relevant to the process of identity stasis occurs when there is a formidable or uncomfortable aspect of particular component of the task at hand, in this case the task being self definition and identification through narrative. This compromised speech can also suggest a flooding of ideas and feelings around a topic. An alternative interpretation is that there is an anxiety associated with speaking in a public space or other self-conscious behavior is present proving an inability to fully verbalize thought as stutter starts and shifting are introduced. However, this analytic perspective, though perhaps contributory, does not fully explain the consistency of the phenomena across data units in relation to Black identity discourse.

In recycling the discourse to make sense of the meaning to the person, additional interpretations of Identity Dilemma Articulation can be found. In the statement, "I think . . . that White people are like the model of success," it is unclear whether "like" is being used as a filler or a qualifier. If a filler, the utterance is simply broken and meaning is not compromised. If "like" is a qualifier, the phrase indicates that "White people are [similar] to the model of success," indicating a model not fully specified within the person's discourse. With further discourse consideration, contextual analysis raises questions as to whether or not the statement is something that the person internalizes, is an attempt to possess agency within a context that is universally imposing and oppositional, or is a reframing of societal expectations. All three analyses find appropriate warranting. Therefore, recycling is emphasized here because of the available interpretations to draw upon in the person's articulation of the Identity Dilemma and the ability to triangulate toward this specific form of identity stasis.

In the next data set, Miles provides further examples of Identity Dilemma Articulation as discursively analyzed.

Miles.session.7: °sometimes when you go like, uh, to White Flynt Mall or somethin', it's just different than going to PG (0.6) when you go, like, certain places. It'll kind of suck the Black out cha though, sometimes. You know sometimes, yeah, it'll feel like, like what you're wearing if you're in a room full of, of other people who are dressed a different way, it don't, it don't feel right. °

Identity Dilemma Articulation is represented in this data set with the person's positioning one ethno-cultural institution against another and discussing dilemma consequences. The bifurcated identification is bound in two, competing mall experiences, "sometimes when you go like, uh, to White Flint mall or somethin', it's just different than going to PG." "White Flint mall" is representative of the white cultural experience and "PG [mall]" represents the Black cultural. The use of the words "its just different" may indicate the presence of affect in the represented Identity Dilemma of difference between distinct cultural environments. The word "different" may indicate an unfamiliarity or lack of comfort that is presumably experienced while not in those "certain places." The polarity explicit in "White Flint mall . . . different than going to PG" and intimated by "different when you go certain places," appears illustrative of the contours of Identity Dilemma bifurcation where there is "different," lack of familiarity or some disconnect experienced in navigating the mainstream and conversely there is sameness and/or familiarity while operating within the Black cultural context. This appears to be reinforced with the discourse, "It'll kind of suck the Black out 'cha."

"It'll kind of suck the Black out 'cha" is the articulated dilemma of maintaining a Black identity while in the mainstream environment of places like "White Flint Mall." "Suck the Black out 'cha" seems to indicate that there is a volume of "Black" that the person possesses that, in some way, can be removed from him depending on how and, "when you go certain places" or the degree to which one is able to successfully negotiate their bifurcated experiences. This "Black" is suggested by the person as the product or essence of the Black cultural experience. Identity Dilemma Articulation, then, is represented in negotiating mainstream identifications that facilitate "feel[ing] different" and Black cultural identifications that allow for fit and a full volume of "Black" to be maintained.

Coltrane further extends the co-construction of identity via Identity Dilemma Articulation with the data below.

Coltrane.session.7: It's just, it feels weird. Like, I feel like, sometimes I can't say what I want to say around white people. Like I just can't (0.3) I don't know, I don't know why, but like I (0.6) don't know, like, I got to act proper. I don't even know why.

That kind of makes it hard for me to like, know, you know, like kind of like who I am, 'cause if I'm putting on a front for (.03) you know, white people or whatever then and then. I just act a certain way when I am with other people you know, it's like (0.3) who does that make me?

"I can't say what I want to say around white people," is a representation of Identity Dilemma Articulation in that there is the bifurcation of identity that suggests that the person, "[can] say what I want to say around [Black] people," but not "around white people" indicating two identities to be negotiated within a universal context of racism.

Interpretation of the active words in this discourse further illustrates the representation of Identity Dilemma Articulation. "Say" is important vocabulary in the discourse because it is representative of expression, an expression that is compromised because something—"white people"—is keeping Coltrane from being "me," signifying the dilemma. "I got to act proper" within the context of the discourse indicates that there is some perceived disconnect between the correct way to act and behavior informed by the person's understood "Black" volume discussed earlier. This consistent negotiation within the data seems to show a consistency of the Identity Dilemma across persons. "Act" could also suggest pretending within the white world with the implicit understanding that there is still the Black cultural to be negotiated.

In the person's discourse there also appears to be the recognition of bifurcated identities to be negotiated, such that the feel[ings] that seem representative of the dilemma and are of substantial focus, can be minimized or channeled differently. The person's desire to do this, to complete or to mature the process of identity stasis by negotiating the bifurcated identities, is found in the discourse, "that kind of makes it hard for me to like know, you know, like kind of like who I am." This data also suggests that the desire to "know . . . kind of like who I am" seems to be impeded by ineffective code switching. The caveat being that there is an indicated realization of "who I am" for the person, on some level, as indicated in his qualifying statement with "kind of like," with his assuming a "Black[ness]" and identifying as such within the context of the focus group sessions.

The person's discourse, "cause if I am putting on a front for, you know, white people or whatever then and then I just act a certain way when I am with other people, you know, it's like who does that make me," is another possible indication of the representation of Identity Dilemma Articulation. The person's "putting on a front," or acting other than who he is "for white people" and "act[ing] a certain," or a more self oriented "way when I'm with other people" seems to indicate a bifurcated identity to be negotiated within a universal context of racism. This is reinforced in interpreting "other people" as being others of color, or at minimum, those who would accept the person, "Black" and all.

"Who does that make me" is indicative of not only of the dilemma of uncertainty with respect to Identity Dilemma Articulation, but also relates a motivation to establish a unified identity. The acknowledgement of the bifurcated identity and a suggested want to unify the "two warring ideals" that have been articulated seems to be an effort to achieve the psychological unity that is central to psychological functioning.

Unadulterated Presentation of Self

Within discourse, the Unadulterated Presentation of Self is a form of identity stasis in which the individual negotiates a need to maintain fidelity to how and who one is within a universal context of racism.

> Parker.session.5: And I just want to prove everybody wrong who believes in the saying of the stereotypical Black man (0.3) cornrows.
>
> You know, prove them wrong, just because of the way that I look, some people have that first sight thought. When they first see you they think that (0.5) they think that they know what you're capable of, but then as soon as you get to talkin' you show them differently. Because you're showing them that you're smart but you're still being who you are (0.5) being who you want to be.
>
> Be who you're comfortable being, like I'm comfortable with the way that I dress and I'm comfortable with my hair style, the way I choose to wear my hair, but I still want to be successful but then (0.5) it's a stereotype of what successful people look like and then it's, it's, it's, it's a stereotype of your average, your average African-American male.

In the person's discourse, Unadulterated Presentation of Self is represented in the negotiation of fidelity in terms of his "dress" and "hair." There is also a sense of agency in maintaining being "comfortable" with his "dress" and "hair." This agency can be interpreted in his use of the word "choose" that is expressed in "how I choose to wear my hair."

It is also important to interpret the discourse in terms of desire to achieve an Unadulterated Presentation of Self that is grounded in the active link between the Black cultural and the mainstream. In his discourse the use of "but I still" may indicate that despite an exercise of choice that may be contradictory to the mainstream, he "still" wants to be "successful." The person extends his thought by suggesting that for him, to "be who you're comfortable being," particularly in terms of a Black cultural physical appearance, can compromise mainstream success. Nonetheless, the Unadulterated Presentation of Self remains paramount.

"Comfort" is conspicuously present and reappears three times within the space of fourteen words. An initial reading and content analysis might suggest that the person is, indeed, comfortable. Additional analysis, however, shows a pattern of overemphasis that points to potential or aspired comfort, but actual internalized discomfort. Data evidence relevant to this point illustrates reframing by Parker where "be who you're comfortable being" could be a positive reinforcement that is contrasted with and then re-presented from "be who you're

[not] comfortable being." This subjective experience of strain and stress, again, represents a negotiation of two identities in an effort to bring a single, unified identity and indicates an Unadulterated Presentation of Self within a universal context of racism that is ever suggesting that to be who he is is to be uncomfortable.

The person's use of the word like is an introduction of the example of what is meant by "be who you're comfortable being." Accordingly, "the way I dress . . . the way I choose to wear my hair" are presented as examples of Black cultural comfort and serve as samples of Black cultural expressions of identity. This interpretation is, again, warranted by the cultural specificity of the clothes that Parker wears and the cornrows that adorn his head.

The Unadulterated Presentation of Self is further demonstrated in the discourse with a representation of twoness indicated where "want to be successful" is followed by "but then" which indicates a rhetorical division and "and then" which further reinforces that division and is grounded in "it's a stereotype of what successful people look like and then it's a stereotype of your average African-American male." The fidelity to how and who one is, persists, then, within the context of the twoness that is present.

The Unadulterated Presentation of Self could also be interpreted as being represented in the person's explanation, "because you're showing them that you're smart but you're still being who you are—being who you want to be." There seems to be a parallel between "talkin" and being "smart" which the person adopts as justification as to why one does not need to change one's "comfort[ability]." This reinforces the interpretation of the person's Unadulterated Presentation of Self that is explained as the ability to maintain relevance and acceptability within the parameters of the full, mainstream society without having to compromise how and who one is considering a universal context of racism.

The Unadulterated Presentation of Self is similarly represented in Wynton's analyzed data passage.

> Wynton.session.5: °When you got a job and people be lookin' at you 'cause you got braids, lookin' at you all weird. So, I mean a lot of people cut their hair, cut their hair low°
>
> Naw, I'd just be myself. I mean (0.5) they should just be able to accept me.

In this discourse there is the positioning of identity against or in opposition to "they," holders of approval or the mainstream, that will not allow the person to "just be his[my]self. I mean they should just be able to accept me." The discourse is perlocutionary, with the speaker presenting a statement to the community of how to maintain within the twoness that he is charged to negotiate. Given that the person has intricate braided patterns as a chosen hairstyle, this exercise in explaining his resolve in maintaining his ethno-cultural style could double as a future reference should he be called to make a decision to modify or to adulterate.

Burden of Proof Assumption

Within discourse, the Burden of Proof Assumption is a form of identity stasis in which the individual negotiates a stereotype imposed by the universal context of racism to confirm or disconfirm as correct or incorrect.

> Max.session.6: 'Cause we always got to work twice as hard to prove them wrong, you know? (1.0) And also it's, like, hard to be yourself and who you are because sometimes (1.2) you have to change it up. Like (2.0) acting different (0.5) you know? (0.5) like (1.0) not say stuff you would normally say.

Burden of Proof is represented in the person's explanation that, "we always got to work twice as hard to prove them wrong, you know?" Here "always" constitutes a time consistency that is never ending and is couched within a universal context of racism. "Got to work twice as hard to prove them wrong" is representative of the need to disconfirm an implied stereotype as incorrect and there is the expression of an exponential effort to demonstrate an ability or validation in the eyes of "them," or those who are assumed to hold the stereotype(s) as accurate. In the discourse, there is not the undoing of racism, but instead the overcoming of racism by being the antithesis of whatever held stereotypically racist position. This effort is expressed in such a manner as to "prove . . . wrong," to demonstrate to a point that previously held interpretations and/or beliefs are incorrect. Interestingly, the negotiating the person is involved in does not center on a need for self-enhancement, rather negotiation and focus is assumed in the work of "proving them wrong."

The unspecified "them" represents those who ascribe to the previously explained "model of success" and, from the person's perspective, can be assumed to be members of the mainstream and/or white people to whom things must be proven. "You know" indicates the desire for validation of a common experience from the other males in the community who are co-constructing this identity with the person; a request for confirmation that his stereotype negotiation is universal among focus group members. Parker's data is, also, in part, an indication of Burden of Proof.

> Parker.session.5: And I just want to prove everybody wrong who believes in the saying of the stereotypical Black man (0.3) cornrows.

> You know, prove them wrong, just because of the way that I look, some people have that first sight thought. When they first see you they think that (0.5) they think that they know what you're capable of, but then as soon as you get to

talkin' you show them differently. Because you're showing them that you're smart but you're still being who you are (0.5) being who you want to be.

Be who you're comfortable being, like I'm comfortable with the way that I dress and I'm comfortable with my hair style, the way I choose to wear my hair, but I still want to be successful but then (0.5) it's a stereotype of what successful people look like and then it's, it's, it's, it's a stereotype of your average, your average African-American male.

Burden of Proof is represented in this person's discourse explicitly, "I just want to prove everybody wrong who believes in the saying of the stereotypical Black man—cornrows." Cornrows are the Black cultural manifestation of the stereotype that the person, wants to disconfirm in the minds of those who "believe[s] in the saying of the stereotypical Black man." In constructing his identity, the discursive analytic process suggests that the person positions himself relative to a universal context of racism and expresses a specific readiness to respond to his position within this context by utilizing himself as the demonstration that will "prove" to others by showing that the larger White world "who believes in the saying of the stereotypical Black man" is "wrong." The language the speaker uses is perlocutionary; it is designed to have an impact on a listening audience that is not there. The speaker is not merely speaking to the other group members, but is creating a relationship with the unidentified missing listener(s).

Though an initial reading might indicate a simple desire to be right, additional analysis of the text suggests more concern for individual virtue as warranted by the choice of content in "want to prove everybody wrong." The pattern is characteristic of a form of identity stasis negotiating that requires the person to accept responsibility for the symbolic representation of all Black people. The person's motive seems to be to symbolically represent himself in a certain way to "everybody who believes in the saying of the stereotypical Black man." The interpretation of this discourse demonstrates the negotiation that the person assumes as a means of reversing the racist stereotype is aimed at that "everybody," that missing listener(s). The person's goal is clear: "to prove everybody wrong." His referential meaning is for the other person and for the group present; his articulation is perlocutionary: his language is designed to impact the listener, but the necessary listener is not there to complete the process. Language in the text begins to function as rehearsal for an event that will allow the speaker to achieve his goal, "to prove everybody wrong."

In recycling the text for exploration of additional representations of the Burden of Proof, the substituted content of the "stereotypical Black man" is a clear self-reference. The physical stimulus of "cornrows" elicits one dimension of the speaker's perception of duality as he continues to articulate from within the Black cultural the external racial response to ethnocentric hairstyle. The speaker's utterance, "believe in" references both a pervasive and entrenched dynamic that may reflect internalization with respect to "everybody[s]" relation to the "stereotypical Black man." The word "saying" indicates another facet of universality that is understood by community, which positions the person within a dichotomous identification because his relationship to the symbolic stereotype is that he has cornrows. This is the physical representation of disconfirmation of the stereotype that he chooses to assume.

FIVE

Beginning

The narratives of the young men in this analysis represent complex identities. This is not ground breaking. The presence of bifurcated identities to be negotiated and brought into balance is also not particularly special. Identities are inherently complex and multifaceted—this is to be expected, perhaps even doubly so for adolescent Black males. The commentary that we extended through the previous tens of pages to now, however, is substantiated with the articulation of constructed identities within context and webbed theory.

The beginning of deep understanding of identities and whole selves rests in our ability to look at the meaning and function of seemingly mundane and ordinary expressions of personality among those who have heavy meaning and purpose tethered to their enactments. Accordingly, the complex, bifurcated identities of these adolescent Black males as represented in their narratives is novel when looking at the meaning and purpose of their formations from an integrated personality perspective. The discourse of the group in this analysis was special in that it, at once, reinforced previous theory of general and racialized identity complexity and suggested that the understanding and representation of this complexity has the ability to free or to fixate one at an identity depending on the person's balance of identity within context. This, again, stresses the core of personality psychology research aims presented previously—pursuit of how the individual person is like all other persons—represented in general identity complexity supported; how the individual person is like some other persons—as supported through racialized constructs that appeared applicable to many within the group; and how the individual person is like no other person, which looks to have footing in future, intrinsic case study (Kluckhohn and Murray 1953; McAdams and Pals 2006).

As documented in Appendix One the young Black males in this sample are normal, some might say exceptional. Their ability to maintain behaviors of normalcy and attitudes toward extended success rest in a realization of who they are relative to one another and in relation to a larger social context that is fundamentally oppositional. There is present in the narratives the working through of identity (Stevenson, McAdams, Allport) toward the goal of integrated selves as indicated by the three forms of identity stasis: Identity Dilemma Articulation, Unadulterated Presentation of Self and Burden of Proof Assumption.

Each of these namings of identity stasis and their support through the discourse of the adolescent Black males engaged suggest a universal goal toward identity equilibrium. Identity Dilemma Articulation is the awareness of a goal to be dealt with. Key in this definition, as was highlighted in the discourse, is an agentic orientation. There is work to be done.

> Max.session.6: (1.0) And also it's, like, hard to be yourself and who you are because sometimes (1.2) you have to change it up. Like (2.0) acting different (0.5) you know? (0.5) like (1.0) not say stuff you would normally say.

The above data segment, part of a larger data chunk in the previous chapter, demonstrates the work. "And it's, like hard to be yourself and who you are because sometimes you have to change it up." Is a universal drive to fit identities into a societal context, one that invariably has a dynamic blending component. The individual impacts the environment, the environment/context the individual and on. "You have to change it up," is code switching, an adapting of identity (personal and/or group) into a congruent, perceived acceptable social identity. That perception, again, part of the interaction of person in context, the figuring of how their self puts forward an identity that links to both the exterior and interior world. Where there is imbalance there is instability within the self, taking a toll on other identities. Ego depletion is then possible and consequent attitude, behavior and potential is compromised because of a psychic tax.

The figuring of how one's self puts forward an identity that links to both the exterior and interior world is a where the expression of personality is like all others. This fitting of identity to society is universal. How it fits narrows to personality expressions that are like some others. The young Black males in the analysis give a look at this through Unadulterated Presentation of Self.

Unadulterated Presentation of Self as presented within the group is illustrative of a group identity, specifically an adolescent Black male group; generally a youth culture group.

> Wynton.session.5: °When you got a job and people be lookin' at you 'cause you got braids, lookin' at you all weird. So, I mean a lot of people cut their hair, cut their hair low°
>
> Naw, I'd just be myself. I mean (0.5) they should just be able to accept me.

The above data segment, again analyzed more fully in the previous chapter, represents a type of personality enactment that the adolescent Black males in the group present as part a collective identity. In fact, the data supports an overlapping instantiation of identity stasis, identity dilemma articulation in the first sentence with the agentic response of Unadulterated Presentation of Self in the remaining text. Presumably, social expectations of conformity for these young men are met with defiance in the choosing to remain in an identified space that is arguably personal identity defined and demonstratively group identity shared as indicated by agreement on and multiple points of discursive congruence with, "I'd just be myself. I mean they should just be able to accept me."

This Unadulterated Presentation of Self and subsequent disconformities are certainly seen in the adolescent B-boy self presentation through slang language and the ubiquitous uniform of baggy pants, oversized shirt, sneakers and a baseball cap balanced justly over a doo-rag. Ironically, this shell often representing a Black identity and cultural fit has come to represent popular youth culture as well, representing conformity within two groups. Again, a fundamental need for balance—stasis—and identity cooperation is present.

Burden of Proof Assumption is the last of the identity stasis forms represented in the identity construction of the Black male adolescents in this text. The push for balance here is found in a need for an individual to demonstrate worth and the validity of a personal identity. Parker illustrates this with:

> Parker.session.5: And I just want to prove everybody wrong who believes in the saying of the stereotypical Black man (0.3) cornrows.
>
> You know, prove them wrong, just because of the way that I look, some people have that first sight thought. When they first see you they think that (0.5) they think that they know what you're capable of, but then as soon as you get to talkin' you show them differently. Because you're showing them that you're smart but you're still being who you are (0.5) being who you want to be.

The above data segment, analyzed in chapter 4, is Burden of Proof Assumption personified. Parker is actively pushing against a society that he positions as consistently devaluing who he is. In a defiance that takes that of the previous example of Unadulterated Presentation of Self further, Parker assumes the responsibility of demonstrating his identity as worthy of not just equity, but praise as substantiated in, "Because you're showing them that you're smart but you're still being who you are being who you want to be." Smart is positioned here as a characteristic or trait that is elevated to respect and admiration, and is integrated into an identity construction that is acknowledged as worthy of the larger social context, an immediate adolescent Black male group and the individual. This type of complex identity representation reinforces the need to look at identity and self complexly.

As discussed in chapters 1 and 2, identity stasis found in the data used suggests the theoretical framework as a process. The process is rooted in McAdams and Pals' (2006) New Big Five mapping. As a result the complexity of identity and the self is situated in a full personality psychology that accounts for identity complexly considering the whole person. In accord with this emphasis, the personality principles of characteristic adaptation, life narratives and the challenge of modern identity and the differential role of culture supported the process of identity stasis. These three principles are evident in an analysis of our participants' movement toward psychological balance through identity construction by way of identity dilemma articulation, unadulterated presentation of self and burden of proof; the three forms of identity stasis analyzed in support of the theoretical and methodological framework. This is a contribution to the understanding of identity as a whole. The racialized form of identity stasis, however, provides further contribution.

Where there was already an understanding of Black identity and personality as complex and multifaceted (Winston et al., 2003; 2006; 2007; Sellers et al., 1997; 1998), a racialized stasis in these young Black adolescent males' narratives extends an interpretation of this race self complexity through an understanding of needed identity balance. The narratives demonstrate a psychological drive toward balance of, at least, two salient identities in an effort to find fit rather than discord within a well defined and well understood social context.

The twoness and negotiation that is foundational in Du Bois' double-consciousness is manifest psychologically in forms of racialized identity stasis that have unique characteristics that can appear as overlapping.

Again, Identity Dilemma Articulation is defined as the recognizing of a twoness to be negotiated by the individual. The Unadulterated Presentation of Self extends this recognition placing agency within the person and responding to the universal context of racism by presenting a self that is uncompromised by the mainstream; in a way, proving to self within society that identifying as Black is important and valid. Similarly, Burden of Proof is the assumption of agency that positions the individual as assuming responsibility for his race and proving to others the validity of their degree of Black cultural identification.

It is important to note that though there were only three forms of identity stasis presented in this research, it is posited that these three represent only those that were warranted and grounded in the discourse, certainly more are detectable with further study.

Racism as a Context for Personality Development

Findings for this analysis also support racism as a context for personality development. Identity stasis is manifest in discourse with the universal context of racism either explicitly or implicitly referenced. This denoted in "Europeans thought they were superior"; "There's been racism since always"; "The first sight thought," positioning and analysis that was of or pertained to a universal context of racism. This support for racism as context for personality development is consistent with arguments made by Jones (2003; 2004) and Winston (2003; 2006; 2007) and is consistent with findings from previous research concerning personality development (Harrell et al., 2003). Nonetheless, research dealing with Black Americans often fail to incorporate this substantiation into theoretical or methodological perspectives. This analytic exercise suggests that failing to do so, particularly in the case of Black American adolescent males, likely distorts research results and analysis.

Race Self Complexity

With the universal context of racism serving as a field within which this sample of Black male adolescents understand who they are, they begin to incorporate and to utilize dynamics of identity balance toward a negotiation of race self complexity. This position that race adds a layer of complexity to the self system of Black Americans (Winston, 2003) is supported in the identity construction of the participants in our sample. There is discourse support for both the biopsychological and cultural historical perspective of race self complexity.

For example, Parker demonstrates a biopsychological perspective in his explanation that:

> Just because of the way that I look some people have that first sight thought. When they first see you they think that, they think that they know what you're capable of.

Parker is addressing his phenotypic visibility and the associated psychological negotiation he must traverse because of attitudes associated with his skin color. As addressed earlier, this negotiation is found in the person's identity stasis representation of Burden of Proof.

The cultural historical perspective of race is similarly supported by group members. One such representation was found in Coltrane's discourse:

> Because, you know, like America doesn't really accept Black people, you know—in that, like since always that's, that's why like there's racism.

Here Coltrane is situating his current identification and identity stasis negotiation within the context of a unique historical experience of Black people of African ancestry in the United States. As a result, in the discourse he reflects the psychological meaning of race that is incorporated into cultured patterns of thought, feelings and actions, and this is represented by his identity construction in Identity Dilemma Articulation. These representations of both identity stasis and race self complexity found in the discourse are additional indicators of theory advancement with respect to how race, from a biopsychological and cultural historical perspective, is understood as part of the psychological functioning of the individual. There is, of course, additional research needed in this area to push theory forward. However, the identity constructions further support identity stasis and race self complexity as viable theoretical constructs.

Identity Stasis Functioning

The identity construction among group members suggests that identity stasis has definite functions. In the following discourse provided by Miles, identity stasis appears as a type of valve by which identification relative to race was positioned such that there is the ability to maintain identity equilibrium and healthy psychological functioning by enhancing and/or shielding identities relative to realities informed by a universal context of racism. The enhancing and/or shielding parallels the universal context of racism's taxing motivations: self protective from racism and self-enhancing one's worth and humanity (Jones, 2003). Though substantiating such a function would require additional analysis and research because of a lack of warranting and grounding for similar representations in multiple identity constructions, the data set is worth consideration.

> Miles: I just don't like school. I, but I want a good job and I like stuff so I know I got to go, but I don't like school
>
> I want my own house, you know what I'm saying. I want, I want a whole lot of stuff. °So I'ma try to go to school. You know, so I can get° a good job and °make that money°
>
> I mean, that's what makes me happy. I like cars. And I like clothes. I like music and all that stuff costs money. (.05) °You need money°
>
> I remember one time when I was real little I went to Connecticut and we drove into like a big open plain where Klansmen came from with torches. And that was scary because they put a cross like right in front of my uncle's house, they burnt the cross, right in front of my uncle's house. I was like four though, four or five. I remember that though. I mean I was, I was little so I ain't really understand it until later on.
>
> I really don't like Black History. As far as hearing about it over, I mean I don't like hearing, like seeing people get lynched on TV or see 'em hanging from trees all the time. That's just depressing to me. I mean, that's depressing. . . . I don't want to sit there and watch that. . . . I don't want to sit there and watch that (1.2) Like my grandmother, she's really into Black history. And she keep getting articles. Like when you drive down the street, on Eastern Avenue and like a mosque or something and they give you the Muslim newspaper for like five cents. And she make you read all that. I mean she used to make me do that when I was little. And I remember each day you know and think that's something for a little kid to see. Seeing you know, Black men on the tree hanging, swinging from a tree. [My grandmother] was like, you know, that's where you come from. I know I didn't want to see that a lot, all the time.

Miles' identity construction in this data passage illustrates the level of complexity within which the process of identity stasis is embedded and as such contributes to race self complexity. On initial reading, there is apparent negation of experienced Black cultural realities. However, deeper analysis of data approached from various portions of the entire identity construction session shows that the person's understanding of Black cultural experiences within a universal context of racism and the acceptance of and overemphasis on mainstream values serve as a protective shield. This defensive process helps in negotiating the emotionally taxing demands for the perceived traumatic experiences that are projected into the person's future as a Black male. This perception of threat energizes his negotiation of two worlds and is grounded in the searing racism that he has witnessed and the lessons he has learned about survival.

Miles introduces his identity construction by explaining, "I just don't like school." It is significant that the culturally normative value implied by school is rejected, while the same culturally normative value of employment: "but I want a good job and I like stuff" is wholly accepted. Interpretation of dynamics utilizing principles of Manichean psychology suggests that materialism is an ethnocultural value that manifests here in mainstream translation. This line of interpretation is drawn upon to characterize actions because it provides a basis for the shared understanding of the group.

Miles justifies his value system in his reference to hip-hop cultural icons "Russell Simmons" and "Bishop Don Magic Juan" in other reported discourse. These examples not only place emphasis on material achievement and possessions, but also symbolically represent conspicuous affluence within culture that is paramount with respect to the Manichean inspired über racism that is part of the universal context of racism the person is charged to operate within. It is also important to note that within the discourse "school" is initiated by the person present tense: "I just don't like school," but then consistently shifts into an ongoing, future experience: "So I'ma try to go to school." This is relevant to identity stasis, because it suggests both the present negotiating of two identities and projects future negotiations as indicated by agency associated with "try."

Thus, identity stasis functioning not only stabilizes in the present, but is available to provide survival for the personality indefinitely. "So I'ma try to go to school" also suggests that the person does recognize and accepts the value in going to school and, implicitly, the value of education.

Miles indicates mainstream emphasis with the discourse of "and make that money . . . I mean, that's what makes me happy." The transitioning from "stuff to money" is a cyclical substitution that functions as reinforcement of a materialism that is highly value-laden. The introduction of "that's what makes me happy" suggests that the pursuit of materialism has a directed purpose of personal reward, "what makes me happy." This becomes an important articulation in analyzing other portions of the person's identity construction and is pivotal in this complex functioning of identity stasis.

The intonation that the person expresses in recall: "remember[ing] one time when I was real little I went to Connecticut and we drove into, like, a big open plain where Klansmen came from with torches" is of critical importance. There is an emotional component to the experience found in the introduction of "scary" into the account. And description of the personal affiliation and relatedness with his uncle suggests, in content, high emotion. When interpreted against the historical symbolism of cross burning, high emotion would be the expected response of his childhood memory of the Klan. Analysis for this data unit requires consideration of repressed feelings as a process. The person offers, "I was like four though, four or five. I remember that though. I mean I was, I was little so I ain't really understand it until later on."

In recycling for deeper analysis "I really don't like Black history," a relatively straightforward statement, indicates that Black history has multiple functions. Black history, in terms of its locutionary or referential meaning, is there for default or escape but is not necessarily what the person is denoting. When interpreted against the fuller repertoire, Black history is for him, in illocution, the connotation of the hostile acts of racism that are associated with the history of Black Americans in the United States. This analysis is grounded in the data, "I don't like hearing, like seeing people get lynched on TV or see'em hanging from trees all the time." Here there are generalities that reflect a personal and collective relationship with "Black history." There is an emotional equating of: "that's . . . depressing" to the history of Black people. This language is substitution for the Black cultural experience. The person distances himself from that identity, perhaps as a means of personal survival or emotional protection. It also seems relevant for discourse analysis, that the speaker positions "that's depressing" in the temporal space of "lynching," a practice that primarily victimized Black males. This would support psychological activity, be it identification with the victim, painful recall of what he: "s[a]t there and watch[ed]" or painful lessons taught by his family.

Miles expands the degree of his discomfort with Black history in his discourse, "and I think that's something for a little kid to see. Seeing you know, Black men on the tree hanging, swinging from a tree." The description of Black men "on the tree hanging, swinging from a tree" adds further grounding to the previous data relating to lynching, a possible distancing and the need to address repressed feelings that might be elicited from the person because of how he considers the violently racist event.

Although the person recognizes the importance of the information shared by his grandmother explaining, "I'm, being older though, it makes more sense," the person defends himself in retrospect in response to the experience(s) as not prepared for the encounter, "and I think that's something for a little kid to see. . . . I know I didn't want to see that a lot." This verbalization of his wanting to avoid these life dealings that are very much related to his personal and collective Black cultural experience serves as an indication of his assuming a version of the "other" identity in an attempt to make[s] me happy. Still, there is an appreciating of Grandmother's . . . Black history as reported with, "I think with I'm being older though, I mean, it makes more sense."

The manifestation of the process of identity stasis in this person's data is more complex than is represented in other data sources. The person recognizes the Black cultural, but ascribes to a more mainstream, Manichean identity. There is no articulation of equal balance. However, there is evidenced identity stasis by way of its complex functioning.

The analytic process of this discourse presents the possibility of the person's choice of wholly mainstream as his effort to reduce internal conflict and to adopt what he sees as satisfaction and fulfillment; the need and/or want to engage in "what makes me happy." This has implications for ego replenishment: he insures that his ego is not depleted, as might have been when having to engage in the types of experiences and associated activities connected to younger racialized events. This appears to represent the functioning of identity stasis as a protective psychological valve. Future studies, however, are necessary in order to provide a more comprehensive, focused attending and warranting of identity stasis as functioning.

Racelessness and Acting White

The functioning of identity stasis also helps to extend thinking related to how and why Black identity is assumed, or not assumed to the extent that some researchers might expect or warrant. There is often presented the concept of racelessness or acting white (Fordham and Ogbu, 1986) in the explanation of the academic achievement gap between Blacks and whites. Here researchers contend that Blacks assume no race or act white in the work to achieve. There is certainly some understanding as to why researches might contend this absent in-depth, integrated analysis. However, in looking at the varied representations of identity stasis among the Black American adolescent males representing in this exercise of identity construction, it appears that a surface non-assumption of Black identity is far more complicated than acting in a particular fashion in order to advance academically.

The psychic energy it takes to assume any of the iterations of identity stasis, identity dilemma articulation, unadulterated presentation of self and burden of proof assumption, is great. In understanding that a primary function of identity stasis might be to serve as defense, the acting white or the racelessness might well be a cognitive negotiation of a universal context of racism that is fundamentally contrary to Black identification. The articulation and/or interpreted manifestation of acting white or not assuming race belies that there is race work and identification being done on another layer informed by race. Considering the ways in which our sample identified and the contextual approach we took to considering their identity development, it seems that a different look at the readily accepted psychological dynamics of racelessness and acting white could help to advance, or at least add texture to the phenomenon.

Approaching from Non-pathology

In a more general sense, this analytic commentary demonstrated particularly important for research in the area of identity and social role because research in this area often occurs within the context of unexplored racism for subject and researcher. Consequently, discursive analysis as a tool proves helpful under such conditions because of its ability to navigate and to illustrate new meanings considering the importance of context. Context is also important in considering analysis relative to participants. In addressing the process of identity stasis and race self complexity there is an understood personality dynamic rather than the assumption of abnormal context. These adolescent males were consistent in demonstrating a pattern of functioning in two competing cultural contexts without the indication of pathology. Identity stasis as a defense, then, does not imply inadequacy, but demonstrates coping and tension-reduction that is practical and productive not pathological and debilitating as is frequently interpreted in participants when looking at race and negotiation.

Further Model Development

With respect to further development of identity stasis and the Stasis/Static Model of Identity Negotiation, there is the need to place greater focus on the functioning aspects of the process, specifically ego depletion/replenishment and other, non-racialized negotiated identities. With a better understanding of these interactions there can be an enhanced ability to understand the coping scaffolding that impacts the dynamics of the model. Also, future studies that look at the process of identity stasis by incorporating self-complexity measures that help to operationalize Linville's (1985; 1987) self-complexity would aid in understanding the Stasis/Static model by outlining how identity stasis interacts with other selves inherent in identity construction.

Also, an instrumental case study approach was most appropriate in pushing identity stasis forward here. An intrinsic analysis has the potential for expanding depth around theoretical and methodological concepts and has the potential for expanding an understanding of identity stasis relative to personality and how individuals represent their innately driven psychological balance.

EPILOGUE

In the fall of 2007 each of the six participants in the focus group sessions that helped to push forward the idea of identity stasis were enrolled in top tier colleges and universities in the South and Northeast. For them this was not particularly extraordinary considering their planning, at least four years prior, to do so. But these young men are extraordinary, as are many unacknowledged Black men in the United States that push, pull and strain against societal definitions to simply be. Not to be superstar entertainers, or even hardcore intellectuals—but *to be*. The work that these young men did and do consistently is dense work of authenticity within a universal context that renders their everyday success of maintaining balanced identities and cohesive selves inauthentic and misfit unless stepping to stereotype. This dynamic is not peculiar to Black males, however.

The complexities of fitting identity to society are daunting and in many effects courageous. And it is done on the daily. Of course, this text was not about success in the conspicuous, rather in the thicket of the rote and seemingly ordinary. Society at large pulls you to it, while identity pulls you to self. There is importance, then, in recognizing the strengths and successes in balancing the two. Identity stasis is positioned, grounded and elaborated here as a psychological attempt to look at the complexities and the successes in balance. Again, Black males were used as a tool at getting to this because of their unique status within the American context. As chapter 5 reinforces, this is the beginning of a program or research that looks to have the capacity to extend in a variety of directions. For now, though, my concern is in what the six have taught me through their identity constructions.

The youngest of the participants in the focus group sessions that framed this analytical commentary entered Morehouse this year. I bumped into him quite by accident during the start of classes, as I'd lost contact with him two years prior. There, in the entrance of the science building where my lab is located, we embraced, went up to my office to talk a bit and I teased him about being in a wack dorm. Then I shared some of the writings in this book with him. In reading his words he whispered, "wow" and nodded slowly in affirmation before we embraced again and he left. I reflected on his simple statement to me before I showed him his discourse: "I've done very well for myself, me and my sister." Absolutely. And it wasn't only about doing well in the sense of persevering and in getting into school, though that was laudable, but about being able to realize his achievement and having the capacity to articulate that self, that space of balanced identity to me and hopefully to others.

He's a good kid—a young man now—they all are. It really is just a matter of being with them, with ourselves, to understand how they are good and how we can capitalize on our strength—whether identity dilemma articulation, burden of proof assumption, unadulterated presentation of self or other.

APPENDIX ONE

Sample and Procedure

The goal of this analysis was to better understand conceptions of identity via, identity stasis and the Black male adolescent. The understanding was framed within and informed by an integrative approach to personality (McAdams and Pals 2006) with special emphasis on the personality principles of characteristic adaptation, life narratives and the challenge of modern identity and the differential role of culture within context.

The tool utilized toward theory and methodological advancement relative to identity stasis was identity construction via life-story narratives. Given the focus on analysis toward theoretical development, the participants were not intended to be representative of a population; they were instrumental. The data generated from a focus group research methodology was situated as a grounded approach with analysis contributing to the development of theory and method of and relating to identity stasis. Accordingly, as a result of purposeful participant selection and absence of statistical representativeness, conclusions and interpretations of data are intended to suggest theoretical generalizations about identity stasis and its hypothesized relationship to theories of personality, identity and self.

Participants consisted of six Black American male students selected from a population of 73 Black American students enrolled in a college preparatory program in the northeastern United States. Students were admitted into the preparatory program based on individual and family interviews that attended to the perspective participant's academic preparedness, motivation, income level and eligibility for college matriculation.

There were several strategies employed to select the six participants in the study. Within the first week of the preparatory program, eight students were selected as possible candidates to participate in a proposed focus group; this was further narrowed to six. Given the focus group research design for this study coupled with discourse analytic techniques to be used, the selection strategy began by identifying individuals who were able to openly discuss their identity and life experiences among an intimate group of peers.

The second strategy for participant selection was to identify six Black American males who presented as different from one another in terms of social and academic experiences and who represented demonstratively different personalities. Although the goal of this analysis was not to examine individual differences in the representation of identity stasis, it was assumed that it would be theoretically interesting and important to try to understand identity stasis as interpreted from the discourse between Black American adolescents uniquely different in their social, academic and personality profiles. To carry out this selection strategy for participants who were uniquely different, initial and follow up interview data from the college preparatory program was used, as well as reports from program counselors and coordinators. Each of the six participants in the case study was given a pseudonym in order to provide confidentiality. The aliases were names of greats.

Participant Profiles

Coltrane is a fifteen-year-old high school junior with a 2.6 grade point average on a 4.0 scale. He attends a prominent private school and feels "pressure to succeed." He appears not to be motivated academically. Rather he seems to be more consumed with trying to understand where he fits socially and how he is going to reconcile stereotypes that he confronts related to what is authentically Black. This is especially salient for Coltrane because of his interest and participation in rowing. He describes this as follows:

> You know, it's like I think, I think you get stereotyped a lot 'cause like we're supposed to play basketball and football and run track just because we're Black and stuff, you know? I mean really that's how I feel. And, I mean, I mean how many Black people do you see doing like cross-country and crew anyway?

In terms of his personality, Coltrane presents as introverted, yet he puts in effort to be funny, telling jokes and making comical gestures. He describes himself as the "nice" one. Coltrane's parents are divorced and he lives with his mother. His father lives in the area but is not fully integrated in his life. He describes as "messed up."

Max is a fifteen-year-old high school sophomore with a 3.57 grade point average on a 4.0 scale. He attends a local public school. His achievement appears to be related to his father's expectations, his sister's high academic performance and his brother's low academic performance. He was born on the western coast of Africa where he lived for seven years. Max describes his family as one that is "strict" and that "demands excellence." In addition to his father expecting him to excel academically, he demands that Max work. Max describes himself as "different" and likes to "think a lot." His father, who appears to be a powerful force in his life, seems to have an influence in shaping how he thinks about his identity. Max describes himself as "quieter" and more contemplative than his father and in constructing his identity, he explains:

> when we had the store and it was getting bad, my father was really stressed out and so it was like a lot of negative vibes coming from him. He was, like, real angry, an angry person who would get loud sometimes. So, man, that's why I'm a calmer person 'cause I was like "that's not for me." I can't be that . . .

Appendix One

Miles is a fourteen-year-old high school sophomore with a 3.13 grade point average on a 4.0 scale who attends a local high school. Although his grade point average is good, he "dislikes school" and is "about that paper" (money). He describes this in:

> I just don't like school. I, but I want a good job and I like stuff so I know I got to go, but I don't like school . . . I want my own house, you know what I'm saying. I want, I want a whole lot of stuff. So I'ma try to go to school.

Miles' family is middle class. In terms of his personality, he describes himself as "funny" and tells a lot of jokes.

Monk is an eighteen-year-old high school senior with a 2.61 grade point average on a 4.0 scale who attends a public school several hundred miles south of the campus where the focus group is taking place. In elementary and secondary school, he describes his grades as "alright."

> I guess I remember going to school, right and I used to, my grades were all right. They were never perfect. You know, I had some flaws. You know, somewhere I could improve, you know?

At thirteen Monk's brother was shot and killed leaving him as his mother's only child. After his brother was murdered, he found life to be "just alright." In terms of his personality, he describes himself as "shy."

Parker is a fourteen-year-old high school freshman with a 2.17 grade point average. Though his grades do not necessarily reflect it, he is a self-described, "academic achiever" and talks a lot about academics:

> Well, I know that in the past two years, like in seventh grade and eight grade I haven't shown it, but still, academics, academics is like all the way, academics. If I don't get good grades then I won't get into college and first of all I have to get into college on a scholarship because my parents can't afford to pay for college for me.

Parker describes his aspirations of success through being "motivated by my father's mistakes." Parker has a younger sister. In terms of his personality, he is reserved, quiet and often soft spoken.

Wynton is a fifteen-year-old high school junior with a 3.2 grade point average. He attends a public school two hundred miles east of the campus where the focus group is taking place. Wynton describes himself as a "pretty good" student and a "baseball player," who wants to play professionally. He has three brothers; two are younger. In terms of his personality, he is ever the optimist, even tempered and respectful of others. The following passage illustrates his disposition:

> I mean like it's, it's hard but it's like stuff you gotta, I mean stuff you gotta deal with. Like there's stuff you can do about it, but you just gotta like take it, keep fighting, keep moving, keep trying to strive toward your goals.

Approach

A case study research method was employed to capture the complexity of identity. Like many case studies conducted within personality psychology, the method used for this study included multiple strategies of inquiry. This multimethod case study approach was adopted in an effort to provide a rich understanding of identity status and identity construction. To capture identity construction in adolescents' discourse, a focus group of the six participants was used. The focus group was also used to gain an understanding of the unique life experiences and representations of those experiences in each participant as a way to understand identity stasis.

Focus Group

A focus group was designed and implemented to capture identity construction in adolescents' discourse, as well as to gain an understanding of their unique life experiences. A focus group is a data collection technique that is widely used in social science, business and various other fields. Within a focus group a moderator directs participants who engage in discussions that are linked to a specified goal or topic. In this analysis, as is similar in most, it was important to acknowledge the relationship between the participants and the group facilitator. This is a dynamic often not reported in psychology, rather in anthropological research and in some areas of educational study (Camic, Rhodes and Yardley, 2003; Denzin and Lincoln, 1999). Nonetheless, it is particularly critical to describe the relationship because of our attending to social context, which in this case has the ability to shape the questions asked, how data is collected, how participants perceive the actual data collection session, the way that the data is interpreted and how it is disseminated and reported.

In this analysis the researcher doubled as moderator of the focus group sessions. In terms of a relationship with the participants, the researcher was engaged in recruiting them into the college preparatory program because of his role as staff in said program. As such there was a certain level of familiarity and ease within the context of the group. Also, this limited pre-existing and sustained relationship allowed multiple looks at the individuals' lived experiences and identifications before, during and beyond matriculation in the college preparatory program.

Discourse Analysis

Discourse analysis is a qualitative research approach developed in social psychology for the study of written and spoken text (Edwards and Potter, 1992; Wetherell and Potter, 1992; Madill and Barkham, 1997; Wetherell et al., 2001).

Discourse analysis is not method only in that it provides an approach concerning a relationship between language and central issues of the social sciences (Wood and Kroger, 2000). This approach, or theoretical perspective, takes a functional view of language by focusing on the way in which it is used to do things such as attribute, persuade and describe. Unlike clinical approaches, description in discourse perspectives is understood as constructed versions of reality rather than as neutral accounts of situations. In detailed analysis of text, descriptions of events, persons and circumstances, there is demonstrated variability and inconsistency. This is regarded as a natural feature of accounts and is used in analysis as a means of assessing how that account functions in its interactional context (Madill and Barkham, 1997).

Discourse analysis is further defined as an analytic commitment to studying discourse as text and talk in social practices (Potter, 1997). The focus is not on language as an abstract entity such as a lexicon and a set of grammatical rules (in linguistics), a system of differences (in structuralism), nor a set of rules for transforming statements (in Foucauldian genealogies). Rather, it is a medium for interaction. Analysis of discourse, then, becomes analysis of what people *do* (Potter, 1997; Wood and Kroger, 2000). It is the study of language with the intent of exploring the use of it within a societal and/or cultural context. The analysis of discourse, then, operates within the domain of critical psychology, in that its approach avoids various epistemological pitfalls of traditional, experimental research. The use of discourse analysis is advantageous in that it moves toward a more inclusive science by utilizing a more inclusive method by partnering with the studied in exploring behavior.

Warranting is the correlate in discourse analysis that addresses traditional scientific inquiry issues of reliability and validity (Wood and Kroger, 2000). Reliability, or the repeatability of findings, is considered a minimal requirement in conventional approaches. For discourse analysis the finding must be stable and repeatable at the level of concept; the instrumental representation of identity stasis, for example. Reliability involves theoretical interpretation in terms of which aspects of an event are significant. Because discourse is socially constructed, the meanings will shift and may be multiple. Also, the warrantability is a co-construction that is not value neutral; rather it is especially valuable.

Psychological studies are increasingly complex and in attempt to address more complex and multi-faceted questions, additional theory and methodologies are created. Discourse analysis speaks to this. Research studies can be divided into three broad categories: quantitative studies, qualitative studies and mixed methods studies. Quantitative studies rely heavily on quantitative methods and statistical significance. Theoretical considerations are posed in terms of a research question and the results of the study are determined by the statistical outcome and how those results reflect the research question. Qualitative research can involve statistical manipulations, but is more concerned with identifying meaning and uncovering substantiation within the context of theory. Mixed methods approaches employ elements of both designs in order triangulate with respect to interpretation of results (Creswell, 2003). In utilizing discourse analysis in this text, the want is to couch our method in the qualitative.

It is important to note the distinction between contemporary discourse analysis and discourse analysis that is focused on racial issues—that is racial identity and racism. Racially centered discourse is especially sensitive to certain standards with respect to what information is determined useful. The interviewee's notions of race and related constructs are oriented to and used in context. In particular it is useful to examine the voice of, or about, "the racial other" as articulated through reported speech and its surrounding context (Buttny, 2003). Stepping beyond the rubric of conventional discourse analysis, racial discourse takes into account the "racial other." This is an important distinction because as Winston et al. makes clear (2004; 2007a; 2007b) race adds another dimension or layer of complexity to the discourse process, influencing theoretical restrictions, interpretation and analysis because of the necessitated incorporation of elements of race discourse and subtle characteristics associated.

There are several key components necessary to conduct an adequate analysis involving racial discourse. As Wetherell and Potter (1992) present them, these components are the discourses themselves, interpretive repertoires, rhetorical construction, interviews and documents, transcription, coding and analysis conventions. An interpretive repertoire can be understood as broadly definable clusters of terms, descriptions and figures of speech often assembled around metaphors or vivid images. In the language of structuralism it would be the system of signification and the building blocks used for manufacturing versions of actions, self and social structures in talk. They comprise part of the resource base for making evaluations, constructing factual versions and performing particular actions. Interpretive repertoires are, essentially, a way of understanding the content of discourse and how it is organized (Wetherell and Potter, 1992). These can be used in tandem with discourse itself in order to analyze racial discourse more fully. Also, analysis should focus on two primary issues: claims warranted and variability. In racialized discourse, such as that associated with identity stasis, the analytic procedure is largely separate from the warranting of claims. How one arrives at a conclusion about what social practices are taking place in a domain of discourse may be quite different from how one justifies that conclusion (Wetherell and Potter, 1992). Variation is key because it "helps the analyst to map out the pattern of interpretive repertoires that the participants are drawing on (Wetherell and Potter, 1992)."

As might be expected, transcription is an essential part of the discourse analytic procedure. Tape and video recordings along with word-processed documentation of sessions conducted offer a multi-level approach to data collection. With respect to transcription, there are several conventions included. Close attention is paid to speech errors, pauses and gross changes of volume and emphasis and in some instances speed breathing and intonation (Wetherell and Potter, 1992). Also items such as sighs, sneezes, clearing of throat and stammering must be of analytic contending. The transcripts should then be coded for easy access and/or understood relative to thematic continuity.

Discourse analysis, again, is situated within the domain of critical psychology. Critical psychologists recognize the methodological problems, or challenges, associated with empirical, quantitative research. Positivism assumes that there is a fixed reality that can be measured by an independent, objective observer. Critical psychologists recognize that the experience of reality is a subjective event and that an experimenter can never really be objective. "Perceptions of reality are viewed through a lens focused by the societal norms and values (McGrath, 2003)."

The theory of discourse analysis seeks to explore the biases that empirical research attempts to eliminate. One of the main strengths of discourse analysis is the way in which the experimenter and participant interact. Often data analyzed comes from transcripts of focus groups (Arminen, 2004) or interviews (Faulkney, 2002). These research settings allow the experimenter to interact with the participant in ways that add depth to data. Unlike the standard psychological experiment, qualitative research utilizing discourse analysis does not attempt to establish causality. The purpose of discursive analysis is to understand more about a phenomenon by studying the multifaceted, dynamic contexts in which human behavior occurs, without the artificiality of a laboratory experiment.

Procedure

Focus Group: The six Black American males selected for this analysis were recruited to participate in a six-person group that met twice weekly for an hour and a half over two months. At the time of recruitment the focus group moderator outlined guidelines for participation and participants signed a consent form that was countersigned by their legal guardian. After an orientation themed session, each participant had a session in which they constructed their life story for the group, with the immediate subsequent session dedicated to time for group responses to the narrative and auto-ethnographic presentation. The orientation session explained the want for the individuals to discuss their lives over the two-month period independently and in conjunction with the larger group. Group participants were also asked to brining any personal devices they thought might give the group a feel and explanation for who they were. Each of the six participants was present for all sessions except for the absence of one member from part of session five and one member from session seven. Each group session was audio and video recorded.

There were two focus group protocols developed and facilitated by a moderator who was trained in group dynamics, group tasking and counseling techniques. The role of the moderator was to serve as a facilitator of the process by safeguarding the best interests of the participants while challenging them to think divergently and introspectively about who they were.

For each of the group sessions a detailed protocol complete with prompts and possible answers to questions posed was used to guide each focus group meeting. The protocols were guides only (Kreuger and Casey, 2000) and except for the first session were informed by the meeting prior in terms of issues shared and emphasized. Protocols for the first two focus group sessions were used as a guide for subsequent sessions.

A cassette recorder with an external microphone and 120-minute cassette tapes were used to audio record the focus group sessions and digital video (DV) recorder, tripod and mini-DV cassettes were used to video record the same sessions.

Video transfer of the recorded data was done from digital video to computer and transcription was done from both video and audio reproductions of the focus group sessions. Two transcribers, one dedicated to each reproduction, transcribed a segment of data and then matched for accuracy. Rules were then devised with respect to how colloquial representations of words, pauses, conclusions, elongation of sentences and word emphasis would be represented in the transcript. These rules were largely based on the commonly accepted core symbols of the Jeffersonian System of Transcription (Sacks, Harvey, Schegloff, Emanuel and Jefferson, 1974) summarized in appendix 2. Once the rules were determined, the focus group sessions were transcribed and when finished, the transcription and the video was cross-referenced to ensure the data was clear, consistent and accurate.

Analytic Strategy, Identity Stasis and Identity Construction

As discussed, discourse analysis is both a theoretical and methodological research approach. What follows is how discourse analysis was employed as a methodological approach in understanding the nature and function of identity stasis as represented in discourse through identity construction. The data that was decided upon for analysis represented those aspects of the individuals' identity construction that directly related to identity stasis. Consistent with the analytic orientation of discourse methodology, the data analysis strategy was iterative and involved multiple and varied levels of analysis.

Level One: Initial Reading: The initial read required the transcripts to be read many times. In addition, the video of each focus group was viewed several times. The purpose of this step in the analytic process was to allow the researcher to assume and to maintain familiarity with the data. Also, after several initial readings of the data, the analytic purpose was to identify segments of data that in any way appeared to represent identity negotiation and racialized, bifurcated identities, the core elements of identity stasis emphasized in this analysis.

Level Two: Selection of Analyzable Identity stasis Data Segments: The segments of data selected were then carefully analyzed to determine if there was a twoness and negotiation that related specifically to Black culture and Mainstream orientations–components of identity stasis.

This analysis provided several data segments that were ambiguous with respect to a representation of negotiation or of a twoess related to Black identity and mainstream identity. For example, it was unclear in one segment if there was a twoness that was a result of a negotiation between mainstream culture and adolescent culture, rather versus Black identity. Due to the ambiguity, these segments were eliminated from analysis for the purposes of this commentary.

Level Three: Identity stasis Naming: At the next level of discourse analysis, the remaining segments of data were used to further the theoretical understanding of a grounded idea of identity stasis. After careful, re-reading of each data segment there was a naming process used to give a conceptual label that could distinguish various forms and functions of identity stasis. The namings were then defined as a formal definition for use at the next level of analysis.

Level Four: Interpretive Discourse Evidence of Identity stasis: The final level of discourse analysis was analytic recycling, scaffolding and reframing in an attempt to closely analyze the meaning and use of words that represented identity stasis. This final level involves analyzing small chunks of the data within segments. This level of analysis comprised the thrust of chapter 4 and provided for data segments in chapters 2 and 5.

With respect to the discourse analytic orientation within which this commentary is framed, validity and reliability surrounding the analysis done is found in the systemization outlined above. Where many studies employ statistical measures as a technique to aid in finding answers to questions (Hinton, 1995), here discourse is used because of the theoretical basis for the analysis. With discourse reliability is found in the ability to detect the repetition in concepts or meanings (Wood and Kroger, 2000) instead of in statistics and replication. Similarly, validity is found in the words used by the person and the common acceptability and warranting of those words in an executed discourse analysis. Therefore, vocabulary, its common usage and the degree to which a researcher is able to warrant the analysis in that vocabulary and common usage is of critical importance in conducting a credible discourse analysis.

APPENDIX TWO

The Jeffersonian Transcription System

[ ]	Square brackets mark the start and end of overlapping speech.
↑↓	Vertical arrows precede marked pitch movement over and above normal rhythms of speech.
Underlining	Signals vocal emphasis; the extent of underlining within individual words locates emphasis, but also indicates how heavy it is.
CAPITALS	mark speech that is obviously louder than surrounding speech (often occurs when speakers are hearably competing for the floor, raised volume rather than doing contrastive emphasis).
°↑I know it°	"Degree" signs enclose obviously quieter speech.
that's r*ight.	Asterisks precede a "squeaky" vocal delivery.
(0.4)	Numbers in round brackets measure pauses in seconds (in this case, 4 tenths of a second). Placed on new line if not assigned to a speaker.
Yeh,	"Continuation" marker, speaker has not finished; marked by fall–rise or weak rising intonation, as when enunciating lists.
y'know?	Question marks signal stronger, "questioning" intonation, irrespective of grammar.
Yeh.	Periods (full stops) mark falling, stopping intonation ("final contour"), irrespective of grammar and not necessarily followed by a pause.
bu–u–	Hyphens mark a cut-off of the preceding sound.
>he said<	"Greater than" and "lesser than" signs enclose speeded-up talk. Sometimes used the other way round for slower talk.

heh heh	Voiced laughter. Can have other symbols added, such as underlinings, pitch movement, extra aspiration, etc.
uh um	How to spell "er" and "erm" the Jefferson way. (Can be added to, etc.)
sto(h)p i(h)t	Laughter within speech is signaled by h's in round brackets.
°°help°°	Whispering—enclosed by double degree signs.
~grandson~	Wobbly voice—enclosed by tildes.
↑↑Sorry	High pitch—represented by one or more upward arrows.
(3.5)	Silence—numbers in parentheses represent silence in tenths of a second.
.shih	Wet sniff.
(.)	A micro pause, hearable but too short to measure.

APPENDIX THREE

Negative Case Analysis

Negative Case Analysis: A data set in which the evidence of identity stasis could not be comprehensively supported from the units evaluated and, thus, falls outside the claims of this research.

> Monk: You know how your brother just beat you up or whatever? You know, you know, I wasn't liking it but, you know . . . it was attention, whatever. And then all of a sudden then he just gone. You know, whatever . . . it's just . . . It's just a hard thing, you know . . . I mean today, it still hurt. . . . And then like the house we was staying in like we couldn't like stay there anymore because it was like whenever the phone ring and everything, we would expect for him to pick it up, you know what I'm saying? Like, you know, there were just so many memories in that house so we just had to move. And I didn't have no choice but to get over it. You know anomy mom so . . . we got over it or whatever, but I mean it start hurtin'. I'm not gonna ever get over it but . . .

Within Monk's identity construction there was an absence of data that strongly supported the theoretical position of identity stasis as a process. Discursive analysis that was drawn upon to explain why the participant did not fall within the scope of the claim upon initial reading suggested that the participant was ostensibly shy and that any experience of identity stasis remained unexpressed. However, in the course of the focus group sessions Monk was very involved in the co-construction of others' identities; this was done through both verbal and consistent non-verbal commitment to the task of the community. And though shy seemed to describe many of Monk's behaviors; he did share very intimate details of his life including race related content. He was clearly a significant part of the focus group community.

In analyzing the identity constructions for content and structure, with respect to Monk, the most important contribution to this work lies in what is absent. The analytic process yields similarity to the overall community: he experiences the world of racism; he understands the responses of others; and he agrees with those entities that more directly support the theorizing with respect to the process of identity stasis. Yet when the full case analysis is drawn upon for evaluation of actions and events for this participant's core construction, it is not grounded in race.

In an analytic interpretation of the data segments, Monk places emphasis on the immediate world of his family and an associated ethno-cultural context. Racism as an overarching reality is neutralized by a family experience and does not require the negotiation of his living in two worlds at this point. Monk lives in one world in a way that is similar to those who do not know racism as their universal context. Examples might be found in those who are developmentally defined by the Nigresence Pre-Encounter stage. Monk represents another example.

The data unit reported above is typical of the participant's identity construction and indicates the traumatic event that impacted the speaker at a young age. The locutionary or referential meaning for Monk immediately connects him to community. What the speaker does, the illocutionary action of the language, moves the speaker into a clinical paradigm of survival and healing. To grasp the nature of discourse, the reality that is constructed here is illocutionary as it functions to help the speaker resolve the long-standing, traumatic issue of family loss; the speaker's language heals. This survival dynamic appears more powerful and immediate than the coping dynamic of identity stasis. The absence of identity stasis in this participant's construction suggests that the process might function as an adaptation mechanism and thus it rises as a process under certain conditions to create stability.

Again the negotiation of two worlds is not the sole identity work for Black Americans. Even though a universal context of racism exists and Black identity of this participant is evident based on the overall interpretive repertoire, the work of identity is different for Monk. This is congruent with the theoretical postulation that though Black identity remains a fundamental of the self-concept and influences related identities; it is not necessarily *the* driving component of a Black American's identity whole. Here extended issues of survival, race and self-complexity seem to most appropriately capture the many-tiered nature of Monk's identity construction.

From the pattern of racial content reported in the data units evaluated, issues of race represent complexity in Monk's identity. However, discursive analysis yields a more central component to this participant's identity construction. Identity work is related to the impacting stimulus of his brother's murder. This does not mean that identity stasis is absent or that racism is negated. In fact, in Monk's identity construction his brother's murder reflects ethno-cultural disparities related to crime and criminal justice. However, for the purposes of this analysis, even in a racist environment, identity stasis is not the only process of adaptation that will be operative, consistent or overt at a given moment for the individual. The instrumental analysis of the focus group yields a sophistication and complexity in the adolescent community that can be reflected in demonstrated identity stasis, but as in Monk's case, can also be reflected in alternative coping skills. At times it becomes pragmatic to frame one's identity and to focus on issues basic to "one world." This immediacy can be recognized clearly when issues of survival become paramount.

In this analysis the process of identity stasis is superceded by a stronger survival and coping need. Monk seems driven to incorporate and to resolve identity issues that emerge from a source of more imposing threat. His mastery of identity issues and family dynamics are grounded intra-culturally. Thus, his emotional availability to negotiate the two worlds, which the case study community embraces, is recognized by the participant, but is not central for him. Moreover, he requires support from his community in order to master the conflict that stems directly from family loss and psychic pain. Again, this intra-cultural work does not negate identity stasis in his world, nor does it negate identity stasis for him as a coping mechanism. His heightened personal concern in this analysis indicates that racism cannot fully define the work for him as a Black American male. The responsibility for Black American males to reach their whole development requires mastery of two worlds; here we see evidence of the work that takes place in one world in the immediate identity work of the participant.

APPENDIX FOUR

Unanalyzed Identity Stasis Representations

Burden of Proof

Coltrane.session.4: I feel like °you know° for me, like, I don't have a choice not to succeed, like, you know, I have to do it °like and feel like° (1.2) I mean I think I'm pretty smart, so, for some reason I feel like I gotta be right, like, when most of the time when I'm talking about stuff, you know? (heh, heh)

I feel like (2.0) in succeeding I can't, you know, be wrong with it, being wrong would be kind of, like, bad . .

Miles.session.5: Yeah, yeah I might, I might throw it up a little. You know, ↑↑good ↑↑afternoon, I'll hook it up to get a job. I would. You see, then, when you get in Russell Simmons position, you could fire the dude.

Miles.session.3: . . . it's just a little bit <u>harder</u> when you are a black male to (0.5) get the good job, to get the real good job and get the good stuff without (1.0) without doing it illegally. Like if I was a like a white man or white boy and then my father owned a real big, maybe, I'm just saying maybe and my father owned a real big business or something and I could just get put on and without even going to college or nothing. And that ain't always the case though but it's a little bit harder

Unadulterated Presentation of Self

Miles.session.3: Like Russell Simmons, you know, he didn't like have to change himself to get to where he is. Like he comes into a meeting with his, you know, whatever he wants on. His cap on, or whatever, he can even wear a baseball cap and stuff. That's cool. To just be able to get there and not have to . . .

Coltrane.session.5: . . . °And he got there by being himself (0.5) you know. He can come into meetings with his Phat Farm hat and stuff. And he runs the meeting.

SELECTED BIBLIOGRAPHY

Akbar, N. 1991. *Visions for Black men*. Tallahassee, FL: Mind Productions & Associates, Inc.

Allen, R. L. 2001. *The concept of self*. Detroit: Wayne State University Press.

Allen, W., and Jewell, J. 1995. African American education since an American dilemma. *Daedalus*, 124, 1.

Allport, G. W. 1937. *Personality: A psychological interpretation*. New York: Holt, Rinehart and Winston.

Allport, G. W. 1954. *The nature of prejudice*. Cambridge: Addison-Wesley Publishing Co.

Appiah, K. A. 2004. Liberalism, individuality, and identity. *Critical Inquiry*, 27(2), 305–332.

Appiah, K. A. 2005. *The ethics of identity*. Princeton, NJ: Princeton University Press.

Arminen, I. 2004. Second stories: The salience of interpersonal communication for mutual help in alcoholics. *Journal of Pragmatics*, 36, 319–347.

Arroyo, C. G. and Zigler, E. 1995. Racial identity, academic achievement, and the psychological well-being of economically disadvantaged adolescents. *Journal of Personality and Social Psychology*, 69(5), 903–914.

Azibo, D. A. 1986. *African psychology in historical perspective and related commentary*. Trenton, NJ: Africa World Press, Inc.

Baldwin, J. 1961. *Nobody knows my name*. New York: Vintage.

Baldwin, J. A., Brown, R., and Hopkins, R. 1991. The Black self-hatred paradigm revisited: An afrocentric analysis. In R. E. Jones ed. *Black Psychology*, 141–166.

Bandura, A. 1986. *Social foundations of thought and action: A social cognitive theory*. Englewood Cliffs: Prentice-Hall.

Bandura, A. 1999. A social cognitive theory of personality. In L. Pervin and O. John eds. *Handbook of personality*, 2nd ed., 154–196. New York: Guilford Publications.

Bandura, A. 2001. Social cognitive theory: An agentic perspective. *Annual Review of Psychology*, 52, 1–26.

Banks, W. C. 1976. White preference in Blacks: A paradigm in search of a phenomenon. *Psychological Bulletin*, 83, 1179–1186.

Bargh, J. A. 1997. The automaticity of everyday life. In R. S. Wyer ed. *Advances in Social Cognition*, 10, 1–61.

Baron, R. M., and Kenny, D. A. 1986. The moderator-mediator variable distinction in social psychology research: Conceptual, strategic and statistical considerations. *Journal of Personality and Social Psychology*, 51, 1173–1182.

Baumeister, R. F. 1986. *Identity: Cultural change and the struggle for self*. New York and Oxford: Oxford University Press.

Baumeister, R. F. 2000. Ego depletion and the self's executive function. In A. Tesser, R. B. Felson, and J. M. Suls eds. *Psychological Perspectives on Self and Identity*. Washington, DC: American Psychological Association.

Baumeister, R. F. 2002. Ego depletion and self-control failure: An energy model of the self's executive function. *Self and Identity*, 1(2), 129–136.

Baumeister, R. F., Bratslavsky, E., Muraven, M., and Tice, D. M. 1998. Ego depletion: Is the active self a limited resource? *Journal of Personality and Social Psychology*, 74, 1252–1265.

Baumeister, R. F., Bratslavsky, E., Finkenauer C., and Vohs, K. D. 2001. Bad is stronger than good. *Review of General Psychology*, 5(4), 323–370.

Baumeister, R. F., Faber, J. E., and Wallace, H. M. 1999. *Coping and ego depletion, recovery after the coping process*. New York and Oxford: Oxford University Press.

Bieri, J. 1966. Cognitive complexity and personality development. In O. J. Harvey ed. *Experience, Structure, and Adaptability*, 13–38. New York: Springer.

Bond, M. H. 2004. Culture and aggression: From context to coercion. *Personality and Social Psychology Review*, 8(1), 62–78.

Boone, S. L. and Flint, C. 1988. A psychometric analysis of aggression and conflict-resolution behavior in Black adolescent males. *Social Behavior and Personality*, 16, 215–226.

Bourdieau, P. 1977. The economics of linguistic exchanges. *Social Science and Information*, 16, 645–668.

Boykin, A. 1977. Experimental psychology from a Black perspective: Issues and examples. *Journal of Black Psychology*, 3(2), 29–49.

Boykin, A. W. 1983. The academic performance of Afro-American children. In J. Spencer ed. *Achievement and Academic Motives*. San Francisco: W. Freeman.

Boykin, A. W. 1986. *The triple quandry and the schooling of Afro-American children*. The school achievement of minority children. Trenton, NJ: Lawrence Erlbaum.

Boykin, A. W. 2003. *The academic achievement of young African American males: Challenges and opportunities*. Achieving and maintaining a balance in the participation in higher education of African American men and women. Washington DC: Howard University.

Boykin, A. W., and Ellison, C. M. 1995. The multiple ecologies of Black youth socialization: An afrographic analysis. In R. L. Taylor ed. *African-American Youth: Their Social and Economic Status in the United States*. Westport, CT: Greenwood Press.

Bradley, C. 2001. A counseling group for African American adolescent males. *Professional School Counseling*, 4, 370–373.

Bradshaw, B. J. 2004. *The color bar: Developing a research tool to examine the psychological significance of phenotypic variation and race self-complexity*. Unpublished thesis. Howard University.

Brewer, M. B., and Gardner, W. 1996. Who is this "we"? Levels of collective identity and self representations. *Journal of Personality and Social Psychology*, 71, 83–93.

Bridglall, B. L. 2004. Mentoring and its role in developing intellective competencies. *Inquiry and Praxis*, 7, 1–4.

Bulhan, H. A. 1985. *Frantz Fanon and the psychology of oppression*. New York: Plenum.

Burlew, A. K. S., and Lori, R. 1991. Measures of racial identity: An overview and a proposed framework. *Journal of Black Psychology*, 17(2), 53–71.

Buss, D. M. 1999. Human nature and individual differences: The evolution of human personality. *Handbook of Personality: Theory and Research*, 31–56.

Buttny, R. 2003. *Talking problems: Studies in discursive construction*. New York: SUNY Press.

Bynum, E. B. 1999. *The African unconscious*. New York: Teachers College Press.

Bynum, E. G., and Weiner, R. I. 2002. Self-concept and violent delinquency in urban African American adolescent males. *Psychological Reports*, 90, 477–486.

Byrne, B., Shavelson, M. and Richard, J. 1996. On the structure of social self-concept for pre, early, and late adolescents: A test of the Shavelson, Hubner, and Stanton (1976) model. *Journal of Personality and Social Psychology*, 70(3), 399–613.

Call, K. T., and Mortimer, J. T. 2001. *Arenas of comfort in adolescence: A study of adjustment in Context*. 1st ed. Trenton, NJ: Lawrence Erlbaum Associates.

Camic, P. M., Rhodes, J. E. and Yardley, L. 2003. Naming the stars: Integrating qualitative methods into psychological research. In P. Camic and J. Rhodes eds. *Qualitative Research in Psychology: Expanding Perspectives in Methodology and Design*. Washington, DC: American Psychological Association.

Camic, P. M., Rhodes, J. E. and Yardley, L. 2003. *Ways of looking at the world: Epistemological issues in qualitative research*. Washington, D. C.: American Psychological Association.

Campbell, D. T., and Fiske, D. W. 1959. Convergent and discriminant validation by the multi-trait multi-method matrix. *Psychology Bulletin*, 56(2), 81–105.

Campbell, J. D. 1990. Self-esteem clarity of the self-concept. *Journal of Personality and Social Psychology*, 59, 538–549.

Campbell, J. D., Assanand, S., and Paula, A. D. 2003. The structure of the self-concept and its relation to psychological adjustment. *Journal of Personality and Social Psychology*, 71, 115–140.

Campbell, J. D., Trapnell, P. D., Heine, S. J., Katz, I. M., Lavallee, L. F., and Lehman, D. R. 1996. Self-concept clarity: Measurement, personality correlates and cultural boundaries. *Journal of Personality and Social Psychology*, 70, 141–156.

Cannon, W. 1932. *The aging of homeostatic mechanisms*. New York: W. W. Norton.

Cannon, W. 1939. *The wisdom of the body*. New York: W. W. Norton.

Carter, P. L. 2000. A review: The role of race and culture in the academic and social attainment of African American youth. *Perspectives*, 65–71.

Carter, R. 1997. *Investigating English discourse: Language, literacy and literature*. New York: Routledge.

Cernkovich, S. A., and Giordano, P. C. 1992. School bonding, race and delinquency. *Criminology*, 30, 261–291.

Chandler, K. 1999. Folk culture and masculine identity in Charles Burnett's to sleep with anger. *African American Review*, 33(2), 299–312.

Chang, S. C. 1988. The nature of the self: A transcultural view. *Transcultural Psychiatric Research Review*, 25, 169–203.

Charlie Rose Show. PBS. New York. 28 Feb. 1998.

Chavous, T. M., Bernat, D. H., Schmeelk-Cone, K., Caldwell, C. H., Kohn-Wood, L., and Zimmerman, M. A. 2003. Racial identity and academic attainment among African American adolescents. *Child Development*, 74, 1076–1090.

Chen, S., Boucher, H. C., and Tapias, M. P. 2006. The relational self revealed: Integrative conceptualization and implications for interpersonal life. *Psychological Bulletin*, 132(2), 151–179.

Chess, S., and Thomas, A. 1977. *Temperament and development*. New York: Brunner/Mazel.

Chess, S., and Thomas, A. 1999. *Goodness of fit: Clinical applications, from infancy through adult life*. London: Routledge.

Clark, K. B., and Clark, M. P. 1939. The development of consciousness of self and the emergence of racial identification in Negro pre-school children. *Journal of Social Psychology,* 10, 591–599.

Clark, S. E., and Groulund, D. S. 1996. Global matching models of recognition memory: How the models match the data. *Psychonomic Bulletin and Review*, 3(1), 37–60.

Cokley, K. O. 2002. Testing Cross's revised racial identity model: An examination of the relationship between racial identity and internalized racialism. *Journal of Counseling Psychology*, 49, 476–483.

Cokley, K. O. 2003. Ethnicity, gender, and academic self-concept: A preliminary examination of academic disidentification and implications for psychologists. *Cultural Diversity and Ethnic Minority Psychology*, 8, 378–388.

Cole, D. A., Martin, Joan M., Peeke, L., Henderson, A., and Harwell, J. 1998. Validation of depression and anxiety measures in white and Black youths: Multitrait-multimethod analyses. *Psychological Assessment*, 10(3), 261–276.

Conchas, G. Q., and Nougera, P. 2004. *Understanding the exceptions: High achieving Black adolescent boys' experiences of school, society for research on adolescence.* Tenth Biennial Meeting. Baltimore, MD.

Corbin, S. K., and Pruitt, R. L. 1999. *Who am I: The development of the African American male identity.* New York: Teachers College Press.

Cosby, W. H., and Poussaint, A. F. 2007. *Come on people: On the path from victims to victors.* Nashville: Thomas Nelson, Inc.

Costa Jr., P. T., and McCrae, R. R. 1992. *NEO-PI-R and NEO-FFI: Professional manual.* Odessa, FL: Psychological Assessment Resources.

Crede, M., Kuncel, N. R., and Drasgow, F. *Study habits, study skills, and study attitudes: A meta-analysis of their relationship to academic performance among college students.* University of Illinois at Urbana-Champaign.

Creswell, J. W. 2003. *Research design: Qualitative, quantitative, and mixed methods approaches.* Thousand Oaks, CA: Sage Publications.

Cronbach, L. J. 1957. The two disciplines of scientific psychology. *American Psychologist*, 12, 671–684.

Cross, S. E., and Markus, H. R. 1999. *The cultural constitution of personality.* New York: Guilford.

Cross, W. E. 1971. The Negro-to-Black conversion experience: Toward a psychology of Black liberation. *Black World*, 20.

Cross, W. E. 1976. The Thomas and Cross models of psychological nigrescence. *The Journal of Black Psychology*, 5(1), 13–31.

Cross, W. E. 1991. *Shades of Black: Diversity in African-American identity.* Philadelphia: Temple University Press.

Cross, W. E. 1998. Black psychological functioning and the legacy of slavery: Myths and realities. In Y. Danieli. ed. *International Handbook of Multigenerational Legacies of Trauma.* New York: Plenum Press.

Cross, W. E. 2004. *Advances in the study of Black identity: Theory and research, society for research on adolescence.* Tenth Biennial Meeting. Baltimore, MD.

Cunningham, M. 1999. African American adolescent males' perceptions of their community resources and constraints: A longitudinal analysis. *Journal of Community Psychology*, 27, 569–588.

Cunningham, M., and Spencer, M. B. 2000. Conceptual and methodological issues in studying minority adolescents. In R. Montemayor, G. R. Adams, and T. P. Gullotta eds. *Adolescent Diversity in Ethnic, Economic, and Cultural Contexts.* Thousand Oaks, CA: Sage.

Curry, G. D. 1992. Gang involvement and delinquency among Hispanic and African American adolescent males. *Journal of Research in Crime and Delinquency*, 29, 273–291.

Descartes, R. 1641. *Meditations on first philosophy: With selections from the objections and replies.* Cambridge: The Press Syndicate of the University of Cambridge.

Devine, P. G. 1989. Stereotypes and prejudice: Their automatic and controlled components. *Journal of Personality and Social Psychology*, 56, 680–690.
Diaz, A. 2005. *Rising to the Challenge: The Children's Aid Society 2005 Annual Report*. The Children's Aid Society.
Dixon, T. M., and Baumeister, R. F. 1991. Escaping the self: The moderating effect of self-complexity. *Personality and Social Psychology Bulletin*, 17, 363–368.
Dixon-Roman, E., Everson, H. T., McArdle, J. J., and Michna, G. A. 2005. *Is the SAT a wealth test? Modeling the influences of family income on Black and White students' SAT scores*. Annual Meeting of the American Educational Research Association. Montreal, Canada.
Dollard, J. 1935. Needed viewpoints in family research. *Social Forces*, 14(1), 109–113.
Dougherty, M. R. P., and Franco-Watkins, A. M. 2002. A memory models approach to frequency and probability judgment: Applications of Minerva 2 and Minerva DM. *Frequency processing and cognition*. Oxford: Oxford University Press.
Dougherty, M. R. P., Gettys, C. F., and Ogden, E. E. 1999. MINERVA-DM: A memory processes model for judgments of likelihood. *Psychology Review*, 106(1), 180–209.
Du Bois, W. E. B. 1897. Strivings of the Negro People. *Atlantic Monthly*, 80, 194–198.
Du Bois, W. E. B. 1903. *The souls of Black folk*. Chicago: A.C. McClurg.
Dyson, M. E. 2007. *Know what I mean: Reflections on hip hop*. New York: Basic Books.
Eccles, J. S., and Wigfield, A. 2002. Motivational beliefs, values, and goals. *Annual Review Psychology*, 53, 109–132.
Edley, N. 2001. *Analyzing masculinity: Interpretive repertoires, ideological dilemmas and subject position*. Buckingham: Open University Press.
Edwards, D., and Potter, J. 1992. *Discursive Psychology*. London: Sage.
Ellison, R. 1995. *Invisible man*. New York: Vintage.
Erikson, E. H. 1963. *Youth: Change and challenge*. New York: Basic Books.
Erikson, E. H. 1950. *Childhood and society*. New York: W. W. Norton and Company, Inc.
Erikson, E. H. 1966. The concept of identity in race relations: Notes and queries. *Daedalus*, 95, 145–171.
Erikson, E. H. 1968. *Identity: Youth and crisis*. New York: W. W. Norton and Company, Inc.
Evans, D. W. 1994. Self-complexity and its relation to development, symptomatology and self-perception during adolescence. *Child Psychiatry and Human Development*, 24, 173–182.
Fanon, F. 1967. *Black skin, white mask*. New York: Grove Press.
Feagin, J. R., and Feagin, C. B. 1996. *Racial and ethnic relations*. Upper Saddle River, NJ: Prentice Hall.
Fiske, S. T. 2004. *Social beings: A core motives approach to social psychology*. New York: Wiley.
Fordham, S. 1996. *Blacked out, dilemmas of race, identity and success at Capital High*. Chicago: The University of Chicago Press.
Fordham, S., and Ogbu, J. U. 1986. Black students' school success: Coping with the "Burden of 'Acting White.'" *Urban Review*, 18, 176–206.
Franklin, A. J. 2004. *From brotherhood to manhood: How Black men rescue their relationships and dreams from the invisibility syndrome*. New York: Wiley.
Franklin, A. J., and Boyd-Franklin, N. 2000. Invisibility syndrome: A clinical model of the effects of racism on African American males. *American Journal of Orthopsychiatry*, 70(1), 33–41.

Franklin, R. M. 2007. *Crisis in the village: Restoring hope in African American communities.* New Kensington, PA: Augsburg Fortress Press.

Freud, S. 1949. *An outline of psychoanalysis: The standard edition.* New York: W. W. Norton and Company.

Garibaldi, A. M. 1992. Educating and motivating African American males to succeed. *The Journal of Negro Education,* 60, 4–11.

Gilbert, G. N., and Mulkay, M. 1984. *Opening pandora's box: A sociological analysis of scientists' discourse.* Cambridge: Cambridge University Press.

Gilmore, S., DeLamater, J., and Wagstaff, D. 1996. Sexual decision making by inner city Black adolescent males: A focus group study. *Journal of Sex Research,* 33, 363–371.

Glass, D. C., and Singer, J. E. 1972. *Urban stress: Experiments on noise and social stressors.* New York: Academic Press.

Glaude Jr., E. 2007. *In a shade of blue: Pragmatism and the politics of Black America.* Chicago: University of Chicago Press.

Gordon, E. T., Gordon, E. W., and Nembhard, J. G. 1994. Pedagogical and contextual issues affecting African American males in school and society. *The Journal of Negro Education,* 63(4), 508–531.

Gordon, E. W. 1995. Culture and the sciences of pedagogy. *Teachers College Record,* 97(1), 32–46.

Gordon, E. W. 1996. Toward an equitable system of educational assessment. *Journal of Negro Education,* 64(3), 360–372.

Gordon, E. W. 1999. The experiences of African American males in school and society. In V.C. Polite and J. E. Davis eds. *African American Males in School and Society: Practices and Policies for Effective Education.* New York: Teachers College Press.

Gordon, E. W. 2000. Production of knowledge and pursuit of understanding. In Carol C. Yeakey ed. *Producing Knowledge, Pursuing Understanding. Advances in Education in Diverse Communities: Research, Policy, and Praxis vol. 1.* Stamford, CT: Jai Press, Inc./Ablex Publishing Corp.

Gordon, E. W. 2001. Affirmative development of academic abilities. *Inquiry Praxis* (2), 1–4.

Gordon, E. W. 2004. Defiance: A variation on the theme of resilience. In R. L. Jones ed. *Black Psychology.* Hampton, VA: Cobb and Henry Publishers.

Gordon, E. W., and Armour-Thomas, E. 1991. Culture and cognitive development. In R. Sternberg and L. Okagaki eds. *Directors of Development: Influences on the Development of Children's Thinking.* Hillsdale: Lawrence Erlbaum.

Gordon, E. W., Bridglall, B. L., and Meroe, A. S. 2004. *Supplementary education: The hidden curriculum of high academic achievement.* Lanham, MD: Rowman and Littlefield.

Gordon, E. W., Bridglall, B. L., and Meroe, A. S. 2005. *Supplementary education: The hidden curriculum of high academic achievement.* Lanham, MD: Rowman and Littlefield.

Gordon, K. 1995. Self-concept and motivational patterns of resilient African American high school students. *Journal of Black Psychology,* 21, 239–255.

Grantham, T., and Ford, D. 2003. Beyond self-concept and self-esteem: Racial identity and gifted African American students. *High School Journal,* 87, 18–29.

Gray-Ray, P., and Ray, M. C. 1990. Juvenile delinquency in the Black community. *Youth and Society,* 22, 67–84.

Greenfield, P. M. 2000. Culture and universals: Integrating social and cognitive development. In L. P. Nucci, G. B. Saxe, E. Turiel eds. *Culture, Thought, and Development,* 231–277. Mahwah, NJ: Erlbaum.
Greenwald, A. G., Banaji, M. R., Rudman, L. A., Farnham, S. D., Nosek, B. A., and Mellott, D. S. 2002. A unified theory of implicit attitudes, stereotypes, self-esteem, and self-concept. *Psychology Review,* 109(1), 3–25.
Grigorenko, E. L. et al. 2004. Alleles of a reelin CGG repeat do not convey liability to autism in a sample from the CPEA network. *American Journal of Medical Genetics,* 126(1), 46–50.
Habermas, T., and Bluck, S. 2000. Getting a life: The emergence of the life story in adolescence. *Psychological Bulletin, 126,* 748–769.
Hammersley, M. 2002. *Educational research, policy making and practice.* London: Paul Chapman.
Harding, V. 1975. The Black wedge in America: Struggle crisis and hope, 1955–1975. *Black Scholar,* 7, 28–46.
Harre, R., and Gillet, G. 1994. *Discursive mind.* London: Sage.
Harrell, J. P. 1979. Analyzing Black coping styles. *Journal of Black Psychology,* 5, 99–108.
Harrell, J. P. 1999. *Manichean psychology, racism and the minds of people of African descent.* 1st ed. Washington, DC: Howard University Press.
Harrell, J. P., Hall, S., and Taliaferro, J. 2003. Physiological responses to racism and discrimination: An assessment of the evidence. *American Journal of Public Health,* 93, 243–248.
Harris, L. 2003. Testing the theory: Cognitive buffers and stereotype threat effects in a Black college environment. Unpublished thesis. Howard University, Washington, DC.
Harter, S. 1999. *The construction of the self: A developmental perspective.* New York: Guilford Press.
Hayakawa, S. I. 1990. *Language in thought and action.* Orlando: Harcourt, Inc.
Helms, J. E., and Carter, R. T. 1991. Relationships of White and Black racial identity attitudes and demographic similarity to counselor preferences. *Journal of Counseling Psychology,* 38(4), 446–457.
Herbert, B. December 26, 2005. A New Civil Rights Movement. *New York Times.*
Hermans, H. J. 1988. On the integration of nomothetic and idiographic research methods in the study of personal meaning. *Journal of Personality,* 56, 785–812.
Hinton, P. R. 1995. *Statistics explained: A guide for social science students.* New York: Routledge.
Hintzman, D. L. 2001. Similarity, global matching, and judgments of frequency. *Memory and Cognition,* 29(4), 547–556.
Horowitz, R. 1939. Racial aspects of self-identification in nursery school children. *Journal of Psychology,* 7, 91–99.
Howard, G. S., Maerlender, A. C., Myers, P. R., and Curtin, T. D. 1992. In stories we trust: Studies of the validity of autobiographies. *Journal of Counseling Psychology,* 39(3), 398–403.
Howerton, D. L., Enger, J. M., and Cobbs, C. R. 1994. Self-esteem and achievement of at-risk adolescent Black males. *Research in the Schools,* 1, 23–27.
Hoyle, R. H., Kernis, M. H., Leary, M. R., and Baldwin, M. W. 1999. *Selfhood: Identity, esteem, regulation.* Boulder, CO: Westview Press.

Hrabowski, F. A., and Pearson Jr., W. 1993. Recruiting and Retaining Talented African-American Males in College Science and Engineering. *Journal of College Science Teaching*, 22, 234–238.
Hutchinson, E. O. 1997. *The assassination of the Black male image.* New York: Simon and Scheuster.
James, W. 1890. *The principles of psychology.* New York: Holt.
Jones, J. M. 1991. The politics of personality: Being Black in America. In R. L. Jones ed. *Black Psychology.* Hampton, VA: Cobb and Henry Publishers.
Jones, J. M. 1997. *Prejudice and racism.* 2nd ed. New York: McGraw Hill.
Jones, J. M. 2003. TRIOS: A psychological theory of the African legacy in American culture. *Journal of Social Issues*, 59(1), 217–241.
Jones, J. M. 2004. TRIOS: A model for coping with the universal context of racism. In G. Philogène ed. *Racial Identity in Context: The Legacy of Kenneth B. Clark.* Washington, DC: American Psychological Association.
Jones, J. M. 2005. Mechanisms for coping with victimization: Self-protection plus self-enhancement. In J. F. Dovidio, P. Glick, and L. Rudman eds. *Reflecting on the Nature of Prejudice.* New York: Blackwell Publishers.
Jones, R. L. 1998. African American identity development: Introduction and overview. In R. L. Jones ed. *African American Identity Development.* Hampton, VA: Cobb and Henry Publishers.
Jung, C. 1921. *Psychology types or psychology of individuation.* London: Kegan Paul.
Kambon, K. K. K. 1992. *The African personality in America: An African-centered framework.* Tallahassee: Nubian Nation Publicationss.
Kardiner, A., and Ovesey, L. 1951. *The mark of oppression.* New York: Norton.
Keita, S. O. Y., Kittles, R. A. 1997. The persistence of racial thinking and the myth of racial divergence. *American Anthropologist*, 99, 534–544.
Kelly, G. A. 1955. *The psychology of personal constructs 1 and 2.* New York: Norton.
Keren, G., and Lewis, C. 1993. *A handbook for data analysis in the behavioral sciences: Stasistical isssues.* Hillsdale, NJ: Lawrence Erlbaum Associates.
Kibour, Y. 2001. Ethiopian immigrants' racial identity attitudes and depression symptomatology: An exploratory study. *Cultural Diversity and Ethnic Minority Psychology*, 7(1), 47–58.
Kihlstrom, J. F., Cantor, N. 1984. *Advances in experimental social psychology.* Burlington: Academic Press.
Kihlstrom, J. F. 2001. The psychological unconscious. In N. K. Denzin and Y. S. Lincoln eds. *Handbook of Qualitative Research.* Thousand Oaks, CA: Sage.
Kihlstrom, J. F., Cantor, N., Albright, J. S., Chew, B. R., Klein, S. B., and Niedenthal, P. M. 1988. Information processing and the study of the self. *Advances in Experimental Social Psychology*, 145–181.
Kluckhohn, C., and Murray, H. A. 1953. *Personality in nature, society, and culture.* New York: Knopf.
Koestner, R., Bernieri, F., and Zuckerman, M. 1989. Trait-specific versus person-specific moderators of cross-situational consistency. *Journal of Personality*, 57(1), 1–16.
Kreuger, R., and Casey, M. A. 2000. *Focus groups: A practical guide for applied research.* Thousand Oaks, CA: Sage.
Kroeber, A. L., and Kluckhohn, C. 1952. *Culture: a critical review of concepts and definitions.* New York: Random House.
Kroger, J. 1996. *Identity in adolescence.* 2nd ed. New York: Routledge.
Larsen, R. J., and Buss, D. M. 2002. *Personality psychology: Domains of knowledge about human nature with powerweb.* New York: McGraw-Hill.

Lee, C. E. 2001. Is October brown Chinese? A cultural modeling activity system for underachieving students. *American Educational Research Journal*, 38(1), 97–141.

Levin, J. 1973. Comparative reference group behavior and assimilation. *Phylon*, 34 (33), 289–294.

Lewin, K. 1946. Action research and minority problems. *Journal of Social Issues*, 2, 34–36.

Liddle, H. A., Jackson-Gilfort, A., Marvel, F. A. 2006. An empirically supported and culturally specific engagement and intervention strategy for African American adolescent males. *American Journal of Orthopsychiatry*, 75(2), 215–225.

Linville, P. W. 1985. Self-complexity and affective extremity: Don't put all of your eggs in one cognitive basket. *Social Cognition*, 3, 94–120.

Linville, P. W. 1987. Self-complexity as a cognitive buffer against stress-related illness and depression. *Journal of Personality and Social Psychology*, 52, 663–676.

Lubinski, D. 1990. Assessing spurious "Moderator effects": Illustrated substantively with the hypothesized ("Synergistic") relation between spatial and mathematical ability. *Psychological Bulletin*, 107(3), 385–393.

Luyckx, K., Goossens, L., and Soenens, B. 2006. A developmental contextual perspective on identity construction in emerging adulthood: Change dynamics in commitment formation and commitment evaluation. *Developmental Psychology*, 42(2), 366–380.

Maddi, S. R. 1996. *Personality theories: A comparative analysis.* Prospect Heights, IL: Waveland.

Maddox, K. B., and Chase, S. G. 2004. Manipulating subcategory salience: Exploring the link between skin tone and social perception of Blacks. *European Journal of Social Psychology*, 34, 533–546.

Madhubuti, H. R. 1990. *Black men: Obsolete, single, dangerous.* Chicago: Third World Press.

Madill, A., and Barkham, M. 1997. Discourse analysis of a theme in one successful case of brief psychodynamic-interpersonal psychotherapy. *Journal of Counseling Psychology*, 44, 232–244.

Mann, D. W. 1992. A mathematical model of the self. *Psychiatry*, 55, 403–412.

Mann, D. W. 1996. Theories of the self. *Harvard Review of Psychiatry*, 4, 175–183.

Marks, B., Settles, I. H., Cooke, D. Y., Morgan, L., and Sellers, R. M. 2004. *African American racial identity: A review of contemporary models and measures.* In R. L. Jones ed. *Black Psychology*. Hampton, VA: Cobb and Henry Publishers.

Markus, H., and Nurius, P. 1986. Possible selves. *American Psychologist*, 41(9), 954–969.

Markus, H., and Wurf, E. 1987. The dynamic self-concept: A social psychological perspective. *Annual Review of Psychology*, 38, 299–337.

Markus, H. R. 1977. Self-schemata and processing information about the self. *Journal of Personality and Social Psychology*, 35, 63–78.

Markus, H. R., and Kitayama, S. 1991. Culture and the self: Implications for cognition, emotion and motivation. *Psychological Review*, 98, 2224–2253.

Marsh, H. W. 1990. The structure of academic self-concept: The Marsh/Shavelson model. *Journal of Educational Psychology*, 82(4), 623–636.

Martin, C., Tenbuelt, P., Merckelbach, H., Dreezens, E., and De Vries, N. K. 2002. Getting a grip on ourselves: Challenging expectancies about loss of energy after self-control. *Social Cognition*, 20, 441–460.

Martin, J. K., and Hall, Gordon C. Nagayama. 1992. Thinking Black, thinking internal, thinking feminist. *Journal of Counseling Psychology*, 39(4), 509–514.

Maslow, A. 1943. A theory of motivation. *Psychological Review*, 50, 370–396.

Maslow, A. 1968. Preface to Motivation Theory. *Psychosomatic Medicine*, 5, 85–92.

Maton, K. I., Hrabowski, F. A., and Schmitt, C. L. 2000. African American college students excelling in the sciences: College and post college outcomes in the Meyerhoff Scholars Programs. *Journal of Research in Science Teaching*, 37, 629–654.

Maton, K. I., Hrabowski, F. A. III. 2004. Increasing the number of African American PhDs in the sciences and engineering. *American Psychologist*, 59(6), 547–556.

McAdams, D. P. 1985. *Power, intimacy, and the life story: Personological inquiries into identity*. New York: Guilford Press.

McAdams, D. P. 1999. Personal narratives and the life story. In L. Pervin and O. John eds. *Handbook of Personality: Theory and Research*, 2nd ed. 478–500. New York: Guilford Press.

McAdams, D. P. 2001. The psychology of life stories. *Review of General Psychology*, 5(2), 100–122.

McAdams, D. P. 2003. *Identity and the life story*. Mahwah, NJ: Lawrence Erlbaum.

McAdams, D. P. 2006. *The redemptive self: Stories Americans live by*. New York: Oxford University Press.

McAdams, D. P., Anyidoho, N. A., Brown, C., Huang, Y. T., Kaplan, B., and Machado, M. A. 2004. Traits and stories: Links between dispositional and narrative features of personality. *Journal of Personality*, 72, 761–784.

McAdams, D. P., and Bauer, J. J. 2004. Personal growth in adults' stories of life transitions. *Journal of Personality*, 72(73), 573–602.

McAdams, D. P., and De St. Aubin, E. 1992. A theory of generativity and its assessment through self-report, behavioral acts, and narrative themes in autobiography. *Journal of Personality and Social Psychology*, 62, 1003–1015.

McAdams, D. P., and Pais, J. L. 2006. A New Big Five: Fundamental principles for an integrative science of personality. *American Psychologist*, 61(3), 204–217.

McCrae, R. R., and Costa Jr., P. T. 1992. Discriminant validity of NEO-PI-R facet scales. *Educational and Psychological Measurement*, 52, 229–237.

McCrae, R. R., and Costa Jr., P. T. 1994. The stability of personality: Observations and evaluations. *Current Directions in Psychological Science*, 6(3), 173–175.

McCrae, R. R., and Costa Jr., P. T. 1997. Personality trait structure as a human universal. *American Psychologist*, 52, 509–516.

McGrath, J. 2003. *Loving big brother*. Oxford: Routledge.

McLoyd, V. and Steinberg L. 1998. *Studying minority adolescents: Conceptual, methodological, and theoretical issues*. Mahwah, NJ: Lawrence Erlbaum.

McWhorter, J. 2000. *Losing the race: Self sabotage in Black America*. New York: Free Press.

Mead, G. H. 1934. *Mind, self, and society*. Chicago: University of Chicago Press.

Miller, P. H. 2002. *Theories of developmental psychology*. 4th ed. New York: Worth Publishers.

Milliones, J. 1976. *The Pittsburgh project–part II: Construction of a Black consciousness measure*. National Institute of Education (DHEW). Washington, DC.

Mischel, W., and Shoda, Y. 1999. Integrating dispositions and processing dynamics within a unified theory of personality: The cognitive affective personality system. *Handbook of personality theory and research*. New York: Guilford Press.

Moore, S. E. 1995. Adolescent Black males' drug trafficking and addiction: Three theoretical perspectives. *Journal of Black Studies*, 26, 99–116.

Moses, C. W. 2006. The African American male initiative: Creating success. *Summary Report of the Study Group of Experts Meeting*. The Children's Aid Society. New York.

Murnane, K., Phelps, M. P., and Malmberg, K. 1999. Context-dependent recognition Memory: The ICE theory. *Journal of Experimental Psychology General*, 128(4), 403–415.

Murray, H. A. 1938. *Explorations in personality: A clinical and experimental study of fifty men of college age.* London: Oxford University Press.

Murray, J. M. 1938. The conscience during adolescence. *Mental Hygiene*, 22, 400–408.

Mussweiler, T., Gabriel, S., and Galen, V. 2000. Shifting social identities as a strategy for deflecting threatening social comparisons. *Journal of Personality and Social Psychology*, 89(3), 398–409.

Myers, L. W. 1998. The effects of urban education on the self-esteem of African American men. *Challenge: A Journal of Research on African American Men*, 9, 57–66.

Myers, L. W. 2000. The academic pendulum and self-esteem of African American male. *African American Research Perspectives*, (Fall), 74–78.

Nagin, R. 2003. State of workforce for New Orleans and the region.

Nasim, A., and Harrell, J. 2003. Racial identity, self-esteem, and academic achievement: Too much interpretation, too little supporting data. *Journal of Black Psychology*, 29(3), 325–336.

Neisser, U., Boodoo, G., Bouchard Jr., T. J., Boykin, W. A., Brody, N., Ceci, S. J., Halpern, D. F., Loehlin, J. C., Perloff, R., Sternberg, R. J., and Urbina, S. 1996. Intelligence: Knowns and unknowns. *American Psychologist*, 51(2), 77–101.

Nelson, T. O. 1996. Consciousness and metacognition. *American Psychologist*, 51(2), 102–116.

Nelson, T. O., and Narens, L. 1990. Metamemory: A theoretical framework and new findings. In G. Bower ed. *The Psychology of Learning and Motivation*, 125–173. New York: Academic Press.

Nghe, L., and Mahalik, J. R. 2001. Examining racial identity statuses as predictors of psychological defenses in African-American college students. *Journal of Counseling Psychology*, 48, 10–16.

Oliver, W. 1994. *The violent social world of Black men.* Lexington, MA: Lexington Press.

Oyserman, D. March 11, 2004. *Social identity and academic engagement: Activating social identity to improve outcomes for low-income minority youth.* Society for Research on Adolescence Tenth Biennial Meeting. Baltimore, MD.

Oyserman, D., Bybee, D., and Terry, K. 2006. Possible selves and academic outcomes: How and when possible selves impel action. *Journal of Personality and Social Psychology*, 91(1), 188–204.

Oyserman, D., Gant, L., and Ager, J. 1995. A socially contextualized model of African American identity: Possible selves and school persistence. *Journal of Personality and Social Psychology*, 69(6), 1216–1232.

Oyserman, D., and Markus, H. R. 1996. *Self as social representation.* New York: Cambridge University Press.

Parham, T. A., and Helms, J. E. 1981. The influence of Black students' racial identity attitudes on preferences for counselor's race. *Journal of Counseling Psychology*, 28, 250–257.

Parham, T. A., and Helms, J. E. 1985. Relation of racial identity attitudes to self-actualization and affective states of Black students. *Journal of Counseling Psychology*, 32, 431–440.

Penuel, W. R., and Wertsch, J. V. 1995. Vygotsky and identity formation: A sociocultural approach. *Educational Psychologist*, 30, 83–92.

Perry, I. 2004. *Prophets of the hood.* Durham, NC: Duke University Press.

Pervin, L. A. 1994. A critical analysis of current trait theory. *Psychological Inquiry*, 5, 103–113.
Pettigrew, T. F. 1968. Intergroup contact theory. *Annual Review of Psychology*, 49, 65–85.
Phinney, J. S. 1990. Ethnic identity in adolescents and adults: Review of research. *Psychological Bulletin*, 108, 499–514.
Phinney, J. S. 1992. The multi-group ethnic identity measure: A new scale for use with diverse groups. *Journal of Adolescent Research*, 7, 156–176.
Pope-Davis, D. B., Menefee, L. A., and Ottavi, T. M. 1993. The comparison of White racial identity attitudes among faculty and students: Implications for professional psychologists. *Professional Psychology: Research and Practice*, 24(4), 443–449.
Postmes, T., Spears, R., Lee, A. T., and Novak, R. J. 2005. Individuality and social influence in groups: Inductive and deductive routes to group identity. *Journal of Personality and Social Psychology*, 89(5), 747–763.
Potter, J. 1997. Discourse analysis as a way of analyzing naturally occurring talk. In D. Silverman ed. *Qualitative Research: Theory, Method and Practice*, 144–160. London: Sage.
Potter, J. 2003. Discourse analysis and discursive psychology. In P.M. Camic, J. E. Rhodes and L. Yardley eds. *Qualitative Research in Psychology: Expanding Perspectives in Methodology and Design,* 73–94. Washington, DC: American Psychological Association.
Potter, J., and Wetherell, M. 1987. *Discourse and social psychology: Beyond attitudes and behaviour*. London: Sage.
Rafaeli-Mor, E., Gotlib, I. H., and Revelle, W. 1999. The meaning and measurement of self-complexity. *Personality and Individual Differences*, 27, 341–356.
Rafaeli-Mor, E., and Steinberg, J. 2002. Self-complexity and well being: A review and research synthesis. *Personality and Social Psychology Review*, 6, 31–58.
Reckless, W. C. 1967. *The crime problem*. New York: Appleton Century Crafts.
Rice, D. W. 2004. Race self complexity: How is double-consciousness manifest in the self-construction of successful African American adolescent males? Unpublished dissertation. Washington, DC: Howard University.
Robins, R. W., Noem, J. K., and Cheek, J. M. 1999. *Naturalizing the self*. New York and London: The Guilford Press.
Robinson, L. 1997. *Black adolescent identity and the inadequacies of western psychology*. Department of Social Policy and Social Work. Birmingham, England.
Robinson, R. 2004. *Quitting America*. New York: Penguin Group.
Rotheram-Borus, M., and Kooperman, C. 1991. Sexual risk behavior, AIDS knowledge and beliefs about AIDS among predominantly minority gay and bisexual male adolescents. *AIDS Education and Prevention*, 3, 305–312.
Rowley, S. J., Sellers, R. M., Tabbye, M. C., and Smith, M. A. 1998. The relationship between racial identity and self-esteem in African American college and high school students. *Journal of Personality and Social Psychology*, 74(3), 715–724.
Ryan, K. E., and Ryan, A. M. 2005. Psychological processes underlying stereotype threat and standardized math test performance. *Educational Psychologist*, 40(1), 53–63.
Ryan, R. M., LaGuardia, J. G., and Rawsthorne, L. J. 2005. Self-complexity and the authenticity of self-aspects: Effects on well being and resilience to stressful events. *North American Journal of Psychology*, 7(3), 431–448.
Ryder, A. G., Lynn E. A., and Paulhus, D. L. 2000. Is acculturation unidimensional or bidimensional? A head-to-head comparison in the prediction of personality, self-

identity, and adjustment. *Journal of Personality and Social Psychology*, 79(1), 49–65.
Said, E. 1978. *Orientalism*. New York: Random House.
Said, E. 1993. *Cultue and Imperialism*. New York: Alfred A. Knopf, Inc.
Sacks, H., Schegloff, E. A., and Jefferson, G. 1974. A simplest systematics for the organization of turn-taking for conversation. *Language*, 50(4), 696–735.
Sarbin, R. T. 1986. *The narrative as a root metaphor for psychology*. New York: Praeger Publishers.
Schmeichel, B. J., Vohs, K. D., and Beaumeister, R. F. 2003. Intellectual performance and ego depletion: Role of the self in logical reasoning and other information processing. *Journal of Personality and Social Psychology*, 85, 33–46.
Sedikides, C., and Brewer, M. B. 2001. *Individual self, relational self, and collective self: Partners, opponents, or strangers?* Philadelphia: Psychology Press.
Sedlacek, W. E. 2005. The case for noncognitive measures. In W. Camaraand and E. Kimmel eds. *Choosing students: Higher Education Admission Tools for the 21st Century*, 177–193. Mahwah, NJ: Lawrence Erlbaum.
Sellers, R. M., Chavous, T. M., and Cooke, D. Y. 1998. Racial ideology and racial centrality as predictors of African American college students' academic performance. *Journal of Black Psychology*, 24(1), 8–27.
Sellers, R. M., Rowley, S. A., Chavous, T. M., Shelton, J. N., and Smith, M. A. 1997. Multidimensional inventory of Black identity: A preliminary investigation of reliability and construct validity. *Journal of Personality and Social Psychology*, 73, 808–815.
Sellers, R. M., and Shelton, J. N. 2003. The role of racial identity in perceived racial discrimination. *Journal of Personality and Social Psychology*, 84, 1079–1092.
Sellers, R. M., Smith, M. A., Shelton, J. N., Rowley, S. A. J., and Chavous, T. M. 1998. Multidimensional model of racial identity: A reconceptualization of African American racial identity. *Personality and Social Psychology Review*, 2, 18–39.
Shavelson, R. J., Noreen M. Webb, Rowley, Glenn L. 1989. Generalizability theory. *American Psychologist*, 44(6), 922–932.
Shelton, N. J. 2000. A reconceptualization of how we study issues of racial prejudice. *Personality and Social Psychology Review*, 4, 374–390.
Showers, C. 1992. Compartmentalization of positive and negative self-knowledge: Keeping bad apples out of the bunch. *Journal of Personality and Social Psychology*, 62(6), 1036–1049.
Shreeve, J. 1990. Argument over a woman. *Discover*, 11(8), 52–59.
Shulman, S., Blatt, S. J., and Feldman, B. 2006. Vicissitudes of the impetus for growth and change among emerging adults. *Psychoanalytic Psychology*, 23(1), 159–180.
Simmons, R. G., Burgeson, R., Carlton-Ford, S., and Blyth, D. A. 1987. The Impact of cumulative change in early adolescence. *Child Development*, 58, 1220–1234.
Singer, J. A. 1995. Seeing one's self: Locating narrative memory in a framework on personality. *Journal of Personality*, 63, 429–457.
Singer, J. A. 2004. Narrative identity and meaning-making across the adult life span: An introduction to a special issue of the Journal of Personality. *Journal of Personality*, 72, 437–459.
Snyder, C. R., and Dinoff, B. 1999. *Coping, where have you been?* New York and Oxford: Oxford University Press.
Solorzano, D. 1992. An exploratory analysis of the effects of race, class, and gender on student and parent mobility aspirations. *Journal of Negro Education*, 61, 30–44.

Spencer, M. B. 1995. *Identity as coping: Adolescent African-American males' adaptive responses to high-risk environment.* Florence, KY: Taylor and Francis/Routledge.

Spencer, M. B. 1999. Social and cultural influences on school adjustment: The application of an identity-focused cultural ecological perspective. *Educational Psychologist*, 34(1), 43–57.

Spencer, M. B., Dupree, D., and Hartmann, T. 1997. A phenomenological variant of ecological systems theory (PVEST): A self-organization perspective in context. *Development and Psychopathology*, 9, 817–833.

Spencer, M. B., Fegley, S. G., and Harpalani, V. 2003. A theoretical and empirical examination of identity as coping: Linking coping resources to the self processes of African American youth. *Journal of Applied Developmental Science*, 7(3), 181–188.

Spencer, M. B., and Harpalani, V. 2004. *Nature, nurture, and the question of "How?": A phenomenological variant of ecological systems theory.* Mahwah, NJ: Lawrence Erlbaum.

Spencer, M. B., Harpalani, V., Cassidy, E., Jacobs, C., Donde, S., Goss, T., Miller, M., Charles, N., and Wilson, S. 2006. Understanding vulnerability and resilience from a normative development perspective: Implications for racially and ethnically diverse youth. In D. Chicchetti ed. *Handbook of Development and Psychopathology.*

Stake, R. E. 1995. *The art of case study research.* Thousand Oaks, CA: Sage.

Steele, C. M. 1997. A threat in the air: How stereotypes shape intellectual identity and performance. *American Psychologist*, 52, 613–629.

Steele, C. M., and Aronson, J. 1995. Stereotype threat and the intellectual test performance of African Americans. *Journal of Personality and Social Psychology*, 69(5), 797–811.

Steinberg, L., Dornbusch, S. M., and Brown, B. 1992. Ethnic identity in adolescent achievement. *American Psychologist*, 47, 723–729.

Stevens, G., and Lockhat, R. 1997. Coca-Cola kids'-reflections on Black adolescent identity development in post-apartheid South Africa. *South African Journal of Psychology*, 27, 250–255.

Stevenson, H. C. 1997. Missed, dissed and pissed: Making meaning of neighborhood risk, fear, and anger management in urban Black youth. *Cultural diversity and Mental Health*, 3, 37–52.

Stevenson, H. C. 2002. Development of the teenager experience of racial socialization scale: Correlates of race-related socialization frequency from the perspective of Black youth. *Journal of Black Psychology*, 28(2), 84–106.

Stevenson, H. C. 2002. Wrestling with Destiny: The cultural socialization of anger and healing in African American males. *Journal of Psychology and Christianity*, 21(3), 357–364.

Stevenson, H. C. 2003. *Playing with anger: Teaching coping skills to African American boys through athletics and culture race and ethnicity in psychology.* Westport, CT: Praeger Publishers.

Stewart, G. August, 1998. *Variations in perceptions of leadership held by IT executives: a qualitative analysis.* Paper Presented at the In Proceedings of the Americas Conference on Information Systems. Baltimore, MD.

Strauss, A., and Corbin, J. 2003. *Grounded theory methodology: An overview.* Thousand Oaks, CA: Sage.

Stryker, S. 1987. *Identity theory: Developments and extensions.* London: Wiley.

Stryker, S., and Serpe, R. T. 1994. Identity salience and psychological centrality: Equivalent, overlapping or complementary concepts. *Social Psychology Quarterly*, 57, 16–35.

Summers, M. F. March 13, 2007. Goal No. 1: Good Science. Goal No. 1: Diversity. *The New York Times.*

Summers, M. F., and Hrabowski, F.A. III. 2006. Preparing minority scientists and engineers. *Science,* 311, 1870–1871.

Tashiro, C. J. 2002. Considering the significance of ancestry through the prism of mixed-race identity. *Advances in Nursing Science,* 25(2), 1–21.

Taylor, C. S., Lerner, R. M., Von-Eye, A., Bobek, D. L., Balsano, A. B., Dowling, E. and Anderson, P. M. 2003. Positive individual and social behavior among gang and non-gang African American male adolescents. *Journal of Adolescent Research,* 18, 496–522.

Taylor, E. D. 2000. Peer support and the academic outcomes of African-American adolescents: A review. *Perspectives,* 25–34.

Terry, R. L. and Winston, C. E. Under Review. *Characteristic adaptations in personality: Multiracial adolescents? patterns of racial self-identification change.* Howard University.

Thompson, C. P., Anderson, L. P., and Bakeman, R. A. 2000. Effects of racial socialization and racial identity on acculturative stress in African American college students. *Cultural Diversity and Ethnic Minority Psychology,* 6(2), 196–210.

Thorne, A. 1995. Developmental truths in memories of childhood and adolescence. *Journal of Personality,* 63, 139–163.

Thorne, A. 2000. Personal memory telling and personality development. *Personality and Social Psychology Review,* 4(1), 45–56.

Thorne, A., and McLean, K. 2000, February. *Contexts and consequences of telling self-defining memories in adolescence.* Paper presented at the Personality Pre-conference, Society for Personality and Social Psychology, Nashville, TN.

Thurman, H. 1998. The search for common ground. In W.E. Fluker and C. Tumber eds. *A strange freedom: The best of Howard Thurman on religious experience and public life.* Boston: Beacon Press.

Triandis, H. C. 1989. The self and social behavior in differing cultural contexts. *Psychological Review,* 96, 506–520.

Triandis, H. C., Bontempo, R., Villareal, M. J., Asai, M., and Lucca, N. 1988. Individualism and collectivism: Cross cultural perspectives on self-ingroup relationships. *Journal of Personality and Social Psychology,* 54, 323–338.

Trice, D. T. June 2, 2006. Cosby needn't look far to find fine Black men, *Chicago Tribune,* 2.

Tyack, D. B. 1974. *The one best system: A history of American urban education.* Cambridge, MA: Harvard University Press.

Tyler, K. M. Under Review. The content of characterization: Towards a model of African American male identity. *Developmental Review.*

Tyler, K. M., Boykin, A.W., Boelter, C. M. and Dillihunt, M. L. 2005. Examining mainstream and Afrocultural value socialization in African American households. *Journal of Black Psychology,* 31(3), 291–311.

Utsey, S. O., Payne, Y. A., Jackson, E. S., and Jones, A. M. 2002. Race-related stress, quality of life indicators, and life satisfaction among elderly African Americans. *Cultural Diversity and Ethnic Minority Psychology,* 8, 224–233.

Van den Berg, H., Wetherell, M., and Houtkoop-Steenstra, H. 2003. *Analyzing race talk: Multidisciplinary approaches to the interview.* Cambridge: Cambridge University Press.

Vandiver, B. J., Cross, W. E., Worrell, F. C., and Fhagen-Smith, P. E. 2002. Validating the cross racial identity scale. *Journal of Counseling Psychology,* 49, 71–85.

Vignoles, V., Regalia, C., Manzi, C., Golledge, J., and Scabini, E. 2006. Beyond self-esteem: Influence of multiple motives on identity construction. *Journal of Personality and Social Psychology*, 90(2), 308–333.
Vygotsky, L. S. 1978. *Mind in society: The development of higher psychological processes.* Cambridge, MA: Harvard University Press.
Wall, B. 1992. *The Rodney King rebellion: A psychopolitical analysis of racial despair and hope.* Chicago: African American Images.
Watson, M., and Protinsky, H. 1991. Identity status of Black adolescents: An empirical investigation. *Adolescence*, 26, 963–966.
Way, N. 1998. *Everyday courage: The lives and stories of urban teenagers.* New York: New York University Press.
West, C. 2001. *Race matters.* New York: Beacon Press.
Wetherell, M. and Potter, J. 1992. *Mapping the language of racism: discourse and the legitimization of exploitation.* New York: Columbia University Press.
Winkler, R. L. Bayesian statistics: An overview. *A Handbook for Data Analysis in the Behavioral Sciences*, 201–231.
Winston, C. E., et al. 2007. Race self complexity: An integrative theory of narrative identity and the psychological meaning of race and ethnicity in American society and culture. Unpublished.
Winston, C. E., and Kittles, R. A. 2005. Psychological and ethical issues related to identity and inferring ancestry of African Americans. In T. R. Turner ed. *Biological Anthropology and Ethics: From Repatriation to Genetic Identity,* 209–230. Albany: State University of New York Press.
Winston, C. E., Lloyd, D., Rice, D.W., Bradshaw, B., and Howard, M. 2004. *Race self complexity and African American adolescents' success: Theoretical considerations for advancing research on identity.* Society for Research on Adolescence Tenth Biennial Meeting. Baltimore, MD.
Winston, C. E., Philip, C. L., and Lloyd, D. L. 2007. Integrating design based research and the identity and success life story research method: Toward a new research paradigm for looking beyond the digital divide and race self complexity within the lives of Black students. *Journal of Negro Education*, 76(1), 31–43.
Winston, C. E., Rice, D. W., Bradshaw, B. J., Lloyd, D., Harris, L. T., Burford, T. I., et al. 2004. Science success, narrative theories of personality, and race self complexity: Is race represented in the identity construction of African American adolescents? *New Directions for Child and Adolescent Development: Social and Self Processes Underlying Math and Science Achievement,* 106, 55–77.
Winter, D. G., and Barenbaum, N. B. 1999. *History of modern personality theory and research.* New York: Guilford.
Wood, L. A., and Kroger, R. O. 2000. *Doing discourse analysis: Methods for studying action in text and talk.* Thousand Oaks, CA: Sage.
Wooffitt, R. 2005. *Conversation analysis and discourse analysis: A comparative and critical introduction.* New York: Sage.
Woolfolk, R. L., Novalany, J., Gara, M. A., Allen, L. A., and Polino, M. 1995. Self-complexity, self-evaluation, and depression: An examination of form and context within the self-schema. *Journal of Personality and Social Psychology*, 68(6), 1108–1120.
Yee, A. H., Fairchild, H. H., Weizmann, F., and Wyatt, G. E. 1993. Addressing psychology's problems with race. *American Psychologist*, 48(11), 1132–1140.
Yin, R. K. 2003. *Case study research: Design and methods.* Thousand Oaks, CA: Sage.

Youngblood, J., and Spencer, M. B. 2002. Integrating normative identity processes and academic support requirements for special needs adolescents: The application of an identity-focused cultural ecological (ICE) perspective. *Journal of Applied Developmental Science*, 6(2), 95–108.

Zimmerman, B. J., Bandura, A., and Martinez-Pons, M. 1992. Self-motivation for academic attainment: The role of self-efficacy beliefs and personal goal setting. *American Educational Research Journal*, 29(3), 663–676.

INDEX

adolescence: narratives, 14; black male, 14–15, 34–36 coping, 25–26; complexity of being, 15–17; model development, 7–9. *See also* Black male, participant profiles

agency, 17, 52, 56–59, 62, 70, 72

analytic Strategy, 86–87

Black male: adolescent, 14–15; culture, 13–14; experience and nature of being a, 12; model development, 7–9; perspective, xv–xvi. *See also* double-consciousness; engagement; participant profiles

burden of proof assumption: defined, xiii, 64, 70; and identity stasis, xii, xiii, 2, 7, 10, 18; supported by discourse, 64–66

context, 17–18, 25, 27, 30. *See also* Field Theory; interpretational analysis; PVEST; Race Self Complexity TRIOS; Universal Context of Racism

coping: Black identity as, 22, 26–29, 44; defined, 26; ego depletion/replenishment, 29–30, 43–44; ethno-cultural, 60–63; graphic models, 45–54; and normal responding, 76; patterns, 22; PVEST, 41–42; self-complexity, 44; and stasis/balance, 11; styles, 29; TRIOS, 42; via defense mechanisms, 27

Cross, William: identity as a social and socialized construct, 10; race, ethnicity and culture, 13; two-factor model of Black identity, 17. *See also* Nigrescence

defiance, 7, 11, 13, 28, 42

discourse analysis: activity, 55–78; defined, 37; and narrative theory, 36–38; overview, 82–85

double-consciousness: defined, xi; and identity dilemma articulation, xiii, 55–62, 70; identity stasis model development, xi–xii, 7, 10, 15–16, 19, 21–22, 25, 31, 35, 39

Du Bois, W. E. B. *See* double-consciousness; twoness

ego depletion/ego replenishment, 7, 11, 29, 35–36, 43, 52–53, 68, 76

engagement, 15–16, 18, 19, 25, 35, 67, 74

existentialism, 12. *See also* engagement

Field Theory, 17, 32, 44

focus group, 18, 55, 82, 85

Goodness of Fit: between person and environment, xiii; from clinical to theoretical, 8–9, 51–54

homeostasis: a theory of equilibrium, 8; psychiatric term, xii; physical science to psychology, 8

identity construction, 7, 10, 12, 19, 23, 29, 34, 36–37, 55, 79, 82, 86–87. *See also* burden of proof assumption, identity dilemma articulation; unadulterated presentation of self

identity dilemma articulation: defined, xiii, 55, 72; and identity stasis, xii, xiii, 2, 7, 10, 18; supported by discourse 55–62

Identity Stasis: defined, xiii, 9–11; forms of, xii, xiii, 2, 7, 10, 18, 55, 62, 64, 70; functioning, 71–75; negative case analysis, 91–93; and a New Big Five, 1, 12, 20, 67, 69; and personality psychology, 1–5, 67, 69; and race self complexity, 1, 44; 46–50; racialized, 28, 31, 43–45; supported by discourse, 55–66; unanalyzed representations, 97

Interpretational Analysis, 16–17

Jeffersonian System of Transcription, 89–90

Manichean psychology, 16, 22–23, 25, 31, 73–74

Multidimensional Inventory of Black Identity, 3
Multidimensional Model of Racial Identity, 39–40
multiple selves. *See* self-complexity
narratives, 7, 9, 14–15, 20, 27–29, 36–38, 55, 59, 67, 69–70, 79, 85
negative case analysis, 91–93
A New Big Five: defined, 20–21; and the contribution of identity stasis, 1; and the process of identity stasis, 69; setting the stage for identity stasis, 12
Nigrescence: connection to identity stasis, 3–4; informing a racialized identity stasis, 40–42. *See also* Cross, William
orchestration: finding balance through discourse, 55–66; and forms of identity stasis, xiii; of identities relative to culture and time, xi; relative to complex negotiation, xv
participant profiles, 80–81
personality, 20–38. *See also* identity stasis, a New Big Five, race self complexity, self–complexity, TRIOS
Phenomenological Variant of Ecological Systems Theory (PVEST), 39, 41–43
Race Self Complexity: defined, 32–34; and identity stasis model development, 40; 46–50; supported by discourse, 70–72
racelessness, 75
racism: defined, 18. *See also* universal context of
resilience. *See* defiance
self, 8–9. *See also* self aspects; self-complexity

self aspects. *See also* self-complexity
self-complexity, 9, 23, 25, 36, 40, 42–44, 48, 78
Stasis/Static Model of Identity Negotiation: description, 7–8; future model development, 78; graphic model, 46–54
Structural Theory, 26–30
Third Eye Model: of identity negotiation, 7; model of identity negotiation, 44–46; of race self complexity, 7
TRIOS Theory: and Black personality, 31–32; defined, 32; and field theory, 32; and race self complexity, 32; and the Stasis/Static Model of Identity Negotiation, 42
Triple Quandary, 21, 22, 23, 32, 39, 43–44
twoness: bifurcated identity, 20, 24, 29, 30, 33, 36, 44, 59–62, 86; negotiation of, 55–66, 70, 87; of identity, 4, 19. *See also* double-consciousness
unadulterated presentation of self: defined, xiii, 62, 70; and identity stasis, xii, xiii, 2, 7, 10, 18; supported by discourse, 62–64
Universal Context of Racism: adolescent expression of identity, 35; a context for personality development, 70; defined, 18; demonstrated through identity stasis and discourse analysis, 55–66; and identity stasis functioning, 71–75; and race self complexity, 71; racelessness and acting white, 75

ABOUT THE AUTHOR

David Wall Rice is assistant professor of psychology at Morehouse College in Atlanta, Georgia. A graduate of Morehouse and of Howard University with a doctorate in personality psychology, Rice is principal investigator for the Identity Stasis Research Laboratory at Morehouse, a research scientist for the Identity and Success Research Laboratory in Washington, DC, and is a research associate of the Institute for Urban and Minority Education at Teachers College, Columbia University. With a masters degree in journalism from Columbia University, Rice has coupled his research with pop culture criticism contributing to *The Source* and *Vibe* magazines and through freelance work that has included commentary for NPR, NBC, MSNBC and written pieces for *The Washington Post*. Rice's research in Personality Psychology is sharply focused on identity and the negotiation of achievement. He consults for a variety of social interest and development organizations, notably among them Gates Millennium Scholars in Virginia, The Children's Aid Society in New York and The W. E. B. Du Bois Society in Atlanta.